Bob Sorge

Author of EXPLORING WORSHIP

FOREWORD BY FRANK DAMAZIO

In His Face

A prophetic call to renewed focus

Oasis House
Kansas City, Missouri

Tenth Printing (2012)

Other books by Bob Sorge:
* *Minute Meditations*
* *Opened from the Inside: Taking the Stronghold of Zion*
* *It's Not Business, It's Personal*
* *Power of the Blood: Approaching God with Confidence*
* *Unrelenting Prayer*
* *Following The River: A Vision For Corporate Worship*
* *Loyalty: The Reach of The Noble Heart*
* *Envy: The Enemy Within*
* *Glory: When Heaven Invades Earth*
* *Secrets of the Secret Place*
* *Secrets of the Secret Place: Companion Study Guide*
* *The Fire of God's Love*
* *The Fire of Delayed Answers*
* *Exploring Worship: A Practical Guide to Praise and Worship*
* *Pain, Perplexity and Promotion: A Prophetic Interpretation of the Book of Job*
* *Dealing With the Rejection and Praise of Man*

Copyright © 1994 by Bob Sorge
Published by Oasis House
P.O. Box 522
Grandview, MO 64030

www.oasishouse.com

Printed in the United States of America
Library of Congress Catalog Card Number: 94-92337
International Standard Book Number-10: 0-9621185-2-4
International Standard Book Number-13: 978-0-9621185-2-4

"One thing I have desired of the Lord, that will I seek: That I may dwell in the house of the Lord all the days of my life, to behold the beauty of the Lord, and to inquire in His temple" (Psalm 27:4).

"And we, who with unveiled faces all reflect the Lord's glory, are being transformed into his likeness with ever-increasing glory, which comes from the Lord, who is the Spirit" (2 Corinthians 3:18, NIV).

I give thanks to God for my wonderful wife, Marci, who has faithfully stood by my side through the longest valley of our lives. Thank you, Sweetheart, for being my best friend.

I thank God for the children He has given me, three treasures: Joel, Katie, and Michael. I pray that our family will continue to grow in the fullness of blessing that comes with beholding His face.

Contents

Foreword 7
Prologue 9

Part One: Pain Management
  1. "Walking Through the Valley" 15
  2. "Passion, Purity, and Perseverance" 27
  3. "The Pruning Process" 37

Part Two: Seeing Jesus
  4. "Hear Him"...49
  5. "A Softened Heart" 59
  6. "In Hollywood's Face" 71
  7. "Take Another Look at Jesus" 77

Part Three: Expressions of Intimacy
  8. "Holy Emotions"..91
  9. "Beholding His Beauty" 99
  10. "The Enemy's Design" 107
  11. "Praise Prayers" 115
  12. "The Flavors of Worship" 127

Part Four: Into His Image
  13. "Adopting a Godly Self-Image"..........................135
  14. "Spiritual Fatherhood" 149

Order Form...159

Foreword

It's not often you can read a modern-day book of Job and come out rejoicing with the sufferer. This is the case with Bob Sorge's honest exposure of his personal walk through the trial of his life and his remarkable responses. What you can expect from this book is:

1. *Blatant Honesty.* We all go through trials, sufferings and contradictions that move us to questioning, doubts, discouragement and even anger.

2. *Painful Reality.* We all have friends or know of people who have a certain physical ailment or terminal disease. We would give anything to see their situation changed. A miracle. A healing. Anything. But with some, nothing changes. They learn to adjust, cope, overcome. Reality of no change is a hard reality to rejoice with. Bob gives us hope.

3. *Godly Perspective.* There is nothing more life-changing than a changed perspective on someone, something or ourselves. The greatest changed perspective is how we see God, understanding Christ and His ways.

4. *Biblical Solutions.* Bob doesn't deal with the typical faith solutions that we so often hear about: Just believe. God will do something supernatural if you just keep praying. Faith always brings healing.

No. Bob deals with painful reality with simple unchanging Scripture. We endure, we change, we find ourselves "in God's face" receiving what we need, not what we want.

Read. Enjoy. Feel the emotions. Ask your own questions. Apply the simple, straightforward solution. Whatever you do, after reading this book make sure you stay "In His Face."

Frank Damazio
Senior Pastor
City Church
Portland, Oregon

Prologue

It all began one Friday in May of 1992. I was speaking at a worship conference in Michigan, instructing the class in the dynamics of using praise as a weapon in spiritual warfare. At the end of the workshop we moved from instruction to practical application, spending some minutes in praising the Lord for His power and authority over those areas where we desired spiritual breakthrough. Then, based upon Psalm 47:1, we closed with a time of shouting to God "with the voice of triumph." We lifted a glorious shout to the sovereign Lord of the universe, exulting in His triumph over the specific areas of challenge we faced.

I shouted with the best of them. We sustained our shout of praise until a sense of completion was shared by the group. Moving from that workshop, I proceeded to speak several more times over the course of the conference. As I returned home to the church I pastored, I felt a soreness in my throat lower down than any sore throat I'd ever had.

The following week the soreness went away. But after preaching in our multiple services the following weekend, the soreness surfaced again. It left that week once more, only to resurface again after a weekend of ministry. By this time I knew something was wrong with my voice, and would have gone to see a doctor immediately except that I had a plane ticket to fly to Singapore the following day for a ten-day ministry trip. By the time I got back from Singapore it felt like a marble was lodged in my throat.

The doctor diagnosed it as an "arytenoid granuloma"—a

"contact ulcer" that had formed on the arytenoid cartilage adjacent to my vocal cords. They ran a battery of tests to try to figure out what caused the granuloma, but found nothing conclusive. We tried some medications and steroids, hoping they could reduce the swelling. Then I took a period of complete vocal rest, but still nothing changed. Finally, in late August of 1992, I had surgery to remove the granuloma.

The doctor assured me that I would be "back in the pulpit" in three weeks, but to the date of this writing I have still not recovered from surgery. Although the granuloma itself is gone, the damage sustained to the arytenoid from the surgery continues to cripple my ability to talk. Although I am comparatively pain-free when silent, it hurts to talk, and the more I talk the more it hurts, to the point that the left side of my neck at times will radiate with pain. And when I do attempt to talk, I have maybe ten percent of my vocal strength. I can be heard from the pulpit if I use a microphone directly upon my lips.

It's bad enough not to be able to talk; but when talking is one's livelihood, one's ministry, one's life — it's devastating. As a pastor, worship leader, conference speaker, husband and father, my life has been traumatized and turned completely upside down by this vocal injury. I do not know how to convey to you in words the kind of emotional upheaval I have known in the past two years — the loss of control, the vacillating moods, the tormenting thoughts, the unending questions, the personality changes, the theological wrestlings, the search for God.

In one sense, this book is the product of all that. I am writing this book from my "cave of Adullam," while in the valley of the shadow of death. There are great things to be learned in the wilderness. God has taught me some things that I want to share with you.

Please do not take the title of this book to be in any way disrespectful toward God. Although the expression "in your face" is sometimes used today in a crude way, that is not the spirit of this book at all. It is with the purest and most upright heart that we come before His face. The title of this book is intended to convey passion, intimacy, and desperation.

Has God been doing things in your life that you don't understand? Have you been crying out to God to bring you into a higher place in Him? Then it's no accident that God has caused this book to be placed in your hands today. May He speak life into your spirit as you position yourself "In His Face."

Bob Sorge
July, 1994

Part One:

Pain Management

CHAPTER ONE

Walking Through the Valley

Yea, though I walk through the valley of the shadow of death, I will fear no evil; for You are with me. (Psalm 23:4)

Imagine that you're Job. In one single day you lose all your cattle, sheep, camels, servants, and children. The cause? Enemy raiding bands, fire from heaven, and a sudden gust of wind that causes the house to collapse upon your children. Like Job, you too would think, "This kind of thing doesn't just happen by chance. There's more going on here than pure happenstance. Something spiritual is behind all this."

I have felt the same way about the circumstances surrounding my vocal injury. My voice was damaged at a time when I was fulfilling God's call on my life to preach. I was lifting my voice in victorious declaration of His sovereignty and power in the earth, and theologically I know of no safer place to be on this planet than when rejoicing in God's sovereign might. The church I pastored had just purchased land for the purpose of building a larger worship facility. The church was growing, the sphere of our ministry was enlarging, when BOOM! All hell seemed to break loose. I don't fully understand why this has happened to me, but I do find myself relating very much to Job's experiences and responses.

What's Going On?

When you go through a hard season, many well-intentioned people try to encourage you by delivering a "word" from God. I've received many "words," and they've run the entire gamut. What has been confusing is that I have received what appeared to be conflicting insight from people whose ministry I honor and who have won the right to speak into my life. One minister said, "I don't see the devil's hand involved here, I see the hand of God in this." Another said, "This is the design of the enemy to shut your mouth."

Then I was reminded that Job's calamity had its origin with both God and the devil. God actually picked the fight, pointing Job out to Satan and saying, "Have you considered My servant Job, that there is none like him on the earth, a blameless and upright man, one who fears God and shuns evil?" (Job 1:8). Satan was fast on his feet and quickly came back with, "Little wonder Job serves You! You've blessed him so much, he'd be stupid not to serve You. But take away Your blessings from his life, and I bet you anything he'll curse You to Your face!" Satan crafted an attack against Job, and God allowed it.

"Is this Satan, or is this God?" The answer just may be, "Yes."

And yet even though Job was under spiritual attack, let me point out that he never once entered into a militant kind of warfare against the enemy. The only one Job ever spoke to, the only one he ever dealt with was God.

There are aspects to my infirmity that certainly appear to have demonic incitement, and yet throughout this season I have had absolutely no militancy in my spirit. I have had only this ongoing sense that my dealings are with God alone.

Lots Of Opinions

When calamity hit Job, his three friends turned into counselors. (When troubles hit your life, you'll never lack for people who are willing to share their wisdom and insight with you.) "God doesn't do this kind of thing to His faithful ones," they said to Job. "This isn't how God treats His saints." There could be only one plausible explanation for

Job's grief, they reasoned. All of their arguments can be boiled down to this one accusation: "Job, there must be some kind of sin in your life." Their counsel was simply, "Repent, and God will restore you."

My study-edition Bible has a center column in it with "cross references" — other Bible references that substantiate the Scriptures at hand. I noticed something remarkable about the counsel of Job's three friends: it is all cross-referenced throughout. Their counsel is substantiated by many other Scriptures. In other words, the counsel they gave Job was scriptural, good, accurate counsel. It was the right counsel — for the wrong situation. It was good advice, but it didn't apply to the situation at hand.

Far too often we are guilty of counseling in the same way. We look at a situation, evaluate it according to our past experiences, and then deliver what we think is good counsel based upon what we see. But Jesus, in contrast, said, "As I hear I judge" (John 5:30). Jesus was saying, "I look at a situation, but then I stop to listen to the Father. What does He have to say about it? When He gives me His perspective on the situation, then I can speak to it and judge it correctly." Job's friends erred because they judged by what they saw rather than by what they heard.

God deliver us of common sense! Far too many Christian counselors rely on their wealth of training, education, and experience when evaluating someone's circumstances. We are doomed to the myopic perspective of Job's three friends unless we first stop, incline our ears to hear what the Father is saying, and then speak accordingly.

A Judgmental Spirit

God has delivered me of a judgmental spirit. Oh, I didn't think I was judgmental. But I realize now that I used to approach some people's problems with a question that had become almost reflexive — "I wonder what they're doing wrong?" A believer whose unbelieving husband was not drawing closer toward the Lord at all... A devout couple who were heartbroken over their rebellious teenager... A sincere father who was constantly struggling to stay afloat financially... In many such circumstances I would find myself, when asked for my pastoral counsel, trying to uncover what was out of order in their lives, what principles they were violating, what they were failing to do. The assumption was, "This heartache has come because of something wrong that's being done, or something right that's not being done."

God has removed that assumption from my heart, and brought me to a new realization that calamity and tragedy come alike to saints and sinners. Just because you're having troubles doesn't necessarily mean you're doing something wrong. Joseph made all the right decisions, and still ended up in the blackness of prison.

In reviewing Job's calamities, I have read many commentaries and heard many messages that have carried this kind of perspective: "Job's problem was such and such," or "When Job finally stopped such and such he was healed," or "This all happened to Job because he feared it would happen," or "God had to empty Job of his spiritual pride before He could heal him." There are many opinions as to what Job did wrong, or was doing wrong, or had to have completed in him before he could be healed. But all those opinions are coming from people who don't understand the book of Job at all, simply because they've never been in that kind of place. Once you've experienced something Job-like, you come to realize what a giant of faith he was. He did great! His responses in the face of overwhelming grief were that of a saint. And yet, the fact that he handled his trials in a godly way was not the thing that brought him deliverance; rather, it was the manifest visitation of God's glory to him.

God didn't come to Job because Job's responses were right; God came to Job because Job cried out to Him. There isn't a right way and a wrong way to cry out to God. Just cry! You need no tips or guidelines, just cry out from the depths of your heart to Him. He hears His children (Psalm 34:15).

The Lord's Discipline

Not all discipline is because you've done something wrong. Hebrews 12:11 reads, "Now no chastening [discipline] seems to be joyful for the present, but painful; nevertheless, afterward it yields the peaceable fruit of righteousness to those who have been trained by it." There are two kinds of discipline.

Some discipline is *punishment*; some discipline is training. Hebrews 12:11 is referring to that discipline of God which is intended to train us in the way of righteousness.

Let's use the example of an Olympic runner. He doesn't come under strict discipline because he's being punished for doing something wrong. He is disciplined because he is striving toward a higher goal. He's not satisfied with being the fastest in the state, or in the nation — he wants to be the fastest in the world. To attain that height requires great discipline.

Some discipline of God is simply because He's wanting to bring you to a higher place in Him.

> *Lord, lift me up and let me stand*
> *By faith, on Heaven's tableland*
> *A higher plane than I have found*
> *Lord, plant my feet on higher ground.*
> [Johnson Oatman, Jr., "Higher Ground"]

Yes, Job was being disciplined. But not because he had done anything wrong. In fact, he had done everything right. (See how God personally attests to Job's righteousness.) But God was bringing Job to an even greater dimension of ministry. His enlarged influence was not confined simply to his generation. Consider how many multiplied generations of saints have been comforted and encouraged by Job's journal of sufferings. Job would have never had that impact over so many millions of holy ones if he hadn't gone through his calamities.

Ups And Downs

The next time you read the book of Job, look at his mood swings. One moment he's in the depths of the valley, fighting extreme depression, venting caustic complaint; the next moment he's on the mountain of spiritual revelation, declaring prophetically, "For I know that my Redeemer lives, and He shall stand at last on the earth" (Job 19:25). Most scholars agree that Job is probably the first book of the Bible written. The height of Job's prophetic insight is more clearly appreciated when we realize that Job had no other Scriptures to stand upon. He was laying the beginning of the foundation of our understanding into God's revealed Word.

I was unprepared for the extreme emotional swings that would take my soul in my times of trial. God has pulled out from under me so much of who I thought I was. "If there's one thing I am, I'm stable." "This much I'm not — I'm not moody." Those proud ideas have been destroyed. Now, when I'm in a place of emotional stability I know it's only because of the sustaining grace of God.

I have come to reali ze that much of the stability we think we have in our lives is nothing but the gracious way God insulates us from grief. God only has to peel away one tiny area of His protection in our lives, and we learn very quickly how empty in ourselves we really are. Not one of us has anything more inherently wonderful about us than does an illiterate, handicapped orphan living on the streets of a city like Rio de Janeiro. The only difference between that orphan and me is the multiplied mercies of God that have surrounded me with so much favor and blessing. It is because we lack this understanding that so few of us respond to the missionary call.

Blessed Be The Name

Sylvia Evans, a personal friend, made a very interesting observation about the book of Job. She said the issue for Job was not depression, self-pity, anger against God, or complaining. The issue in his life was blessing or cursing. Would he bless or curse God? The devil wagered that Job would curse God, and Job's own wife goaded him to do just that. But instead Job said, "The Lord gave, and the Lord has taken away; blessed be the name of the Lord" (Job 1:21). When Sylvia recently asked me if I had cursed God yet, I was thankful that I could say "No."

"Blessed be the name of the Lord." His name represents His character — who He is. When I was in one of my emotional valleys, that phrase meant a lot to me. I wanted to worship the Lord, but just couldn't find it within myself to bless Him for my present circumstances. Struggling to come to terms with that, I was reminded that Job didn't extol the ways of God. He didn't bless God's *works*, because at that point in his life he couldn't. But he could extol the *name* of the Lord. Then I realized that I could too. I know that life's challenges can become so difficult at times that we don't feel like blessing God's ways or works. But I have discovered that no matter how difficult things get, I can always bless the name of the Lord. "The name of the Lord is a strong tower; The righteous run to it and are safe" (Proverbs 18:10). Take refuge, war-weary saint, in the name of the Lord.

In His Face

The Lord has shown me the key to Job's salvation, the thing that brought him through to the other side. Despite all his wrestlings, his questions, his anger, his self-pity, his depression and his indignation, *he kept his face toward God.* You can get away with almost anything if you do it in the face of God. (Please do not misunderstand me, I am not saying you can get away with moral failure or outright sin.) You can rant, you can rave, you can kick, you can yell, you can have a temper tantrum, you can have a pity-party, as long as you do it in God's face. I'm not saying it's okay to do those things; but I am saying that if you do them in the face of God, He will bring you through.

The Lord rebuked His people through the prophet Hosea because they were wailing and mourning, but they were not crying out to Him. "They did not cry out to Me with their heart when they wailed upon their beds" (Hosea 7:14). If you're hurting, it is eternally important the direction you choose to aim your painful cries. It's not enough to cry out — you must cry out *to the Lord.*

I discovered an intriguing definition of unbelief based upon Hebrews 3:12, "Beware, brethren, lest there be in any of you an evil heart of unbelief in departing from the living God." In the sense of that verse, unbelief is "turning away from God." Conversely then, faith is "staying in the face of God." When you're in the furnace of affliction, sometimes the only expression of faith you can muster is that of placing yourself in the face of God.

Job kept his face toward God, and in time God came to him. Beloved, in time He'll meet you too.

The Psalmist Anointing

In my months of turmoil I have found great strength and consolation in the Psalms. It wasn't until my season of calamity that I realized how many of the Psalms were written from a place of depression, despair, and grief. David has suddenly become a man I can relate to very personally.

I asked, "Lord, give me the heart of a psalmist." I thought that was a nice thing to ask for. You know, psalmists get on the keyboard, the music flows, the anointing comes down, everybody melts in the presence of God, new songs are birthed — it's great being a psalmist. But it's only been recently that entire portions of the Psalms have come alive to me. I used to read certain Psalms and think to myself, "I don't relate." I couldn't relate to statements like, "My tears are my food day and night." Until now. I wanted to have the heart of a psalmist, but I didn't like the way it came.

Shortly before my infirmity struck, the Lord prompted me to read "a Psalm a day." I know folks who read one chapter from the Book of Proverbs each day; but the Lord whispered in my heart that if I want to have the psalmist anointing, I need to hang out with the psalmists. That practice of living daily in the Psalms has been a source of immeasurable comfort and sustenance to me in times of darkness. Many of the Psalms are the chronicles of men who in times of great personal pain cried out — but they cried out *in the face of God.*

Valley Of Baca

Let me direct your attention for a moment to Psalm 84:5-6: "Blessed is the man whose strength is in You, whose heart is set on pilgrimage. As they pass through the Valley of Baca, they make it a spring; the rain also covers it with pools."

The Valley of Baca is a desert valley, and the Baca plant is a kind of plant that can survive in dry conditions. "Baca" means "Weeping," and when you go through the desert valley you truly do fill it with tears of weeping. But for the first time I connected this verse on the Valley of Baca with the verse immediately following it: "They go from strength to strength; each one appears before God in Zion" (Psalm 84:7).

"Strength" coincides for me with the mountaintop, so that I would paraphrase the verse to say, "They go from mountaintop to mountaintop." I had always envisioned the believer moving from mountaintop to mountaintop "gondola style," being carried from one peak to the next. I could see the mighty man of God leaping, as it were, from one mountain peak of glorious victory to another. But verse six brings harsh reality to bear on that shimmering mirage: between every two mountains is a valley. So the Christian walk is not pictured in this text as "mountaintop to mountaintop," rather it is "mountaintop to valley, to mountaintop, to valley."

I would like to apply this principle to two similar expressions in the Bible — "faith to faith" (Romans 1:17) and "glory to glory" (2 Corinthians 3:18). Could it possibly be that the process of "faith to faith" is actually a moving from one mountaintop of faith, through a valley of struggle and doubt and questioning, to another mountaintop of even greater faith? And could it possibly be that the process of "glory to glory" is actually a progression from one mountaintop of glory, through a valley of things somewhat inglorious, to yet another mountaintop of even greater glory? Many saints have discovered that some of their greatest attainments in God have been preceded by some of their lowest valleys.

If all this is true, then it gives me the freedom to have seasons of struggle. If I see a brother in calamity, I can stand with him in it, knowing that God has a purpose in this season. In some systems of biblical interpretation, believers don't have the option to go through times of struggle, confusion, discouragement, perplexity, or grief. But the Bible is full of the stories of men and women of God who went through dark seasons that were specifically intended by God to be just that. (I address this more fully in Chapter Fourteen.)

I use the word "season" purposefully here, because I don't believe God intends for darkness and struggle and difficulty to be our lifelong experience. God may lead us into a valley of despair for a season, but the Scripture testifies, "Yea, though I walk *through* the valley of the shadow of death" (Psalm 23:4). God doesn't lead us into valleys to leave us there, but to bring us through.

Asking Questions

I have been very comforted by Psalm 27:4, "One thing I have desired of the Lord, that will I seek: That I may dwell in the house of the Lord all the days of my life, to behold the beauty of the Lord, and to inquire in His temple." I want to point to the invitation in the last phrase of that verse, "and to inquire in His temple." It is an invitation to come into His presence for the purpose of questioning, asking, inquiring, searching out. Perhaps you've heard it said, "Don't question God," or, "A Christian should never ask why." But that's not how I read this Scripture. I see this verse inviting us to bring our questions. Have you ever wondered, "God, what is happening to me?" "Lord, what are you doing in my life?" Bring those questions into His temple, and ask.

Our problem is, we bring our questions, then turn to our neighbor and start to bicker about God. "I don't understand why God is doing this to me." Don't turn; that's unbelief. It's very important where you take your questions. The invitation is to bring your questions into His presence, and inquire of Him *in His face*.

Standing

Recently I said to God, "Lord, I've done everything I know to do. I've prayed, I've praised, I've repented, I've fasted, I've rebuked, I've surrendered, I've read books, I've quoted Scriptures, I've spent time in Your presence, I've reconciled with everyone I could conceive had a problem with me, I've gone on an extended personal retreat in solitude. I don't know of anything else to do."

The next morning I awoke and this verse was whispered gently into my heart, "and having done all, to stand" (Ephesians 6:13). I felt like I didn't have strength to do anything else, but yes, I could still stand. People would ask me, "How are you doing?" and my answer was, "Standing."

Some victories are gained not through an aggressive posturing of faith, but by simply standing. God didn't deliver Joseph from his prison because Joseph had a dynamic stance of faith, but because he kept his gaze fixed upon God. Joseph didn't understand what was happening to him. He could get powerful revelations for other people (the butler and the baker), but when it came to his own life he could see nothing. But at the right time God came and delivered him. "The Lord...does not despise His prisoners" (Psalm 69:33).

Let me tell you how to stand: Stand like Job and Joseph — in the face of God.

CHAPTER TWO

Passion, Purity & Perseverance

These three words — passion, purity, and perseverance — represent principles that are of crucial significance for those who desire to abide in the face of God.

1. Passion

God is not trying to grow a following of pew-sitters who know how to visit Him on weekends. No, He's raising up an army of passionate worshipers who desire above all else to live in the radiance of His countenance.

Have you marvelled at the eruption of worship that has exploded throughout the nations in recent years? Multiple millions of worship cassettes have been sent literally around the globe. A song of passionate praise has filled the mouths of God's people. But why? And why now? The answer lies in the fact that the end-time harvest will be gathered by a host of singing soulwinners who are consumed with a passion for Jesus.

A Passion To Be With Him

What a day to be alive — breakfast in Baltimore, lunch in Little Rock, baggage in Boston. Never before have people been beset with so many demands pulling incessantly on their time and attention. In this day and age, the only way we'll find time to be with God will be if we have a longing for His presence that can't be satisfied with any substitute.

I'm wondering if you've come to the place of such passion and desire for Jesus that your chest literally heaves as you long for Him. "As the deer pants for the water brooks, so pants my soul for You, O God" (Psalm 42:1).

Being the author of the book *Exploring Worship*, I am frequently asked, "What do you see the Lord doing in the church these days in the area of praise and worship?" The best answer I have is that God is calling us to a renewed simplicity of focus on the person of Jesus. That includes, I believe, a return to the cross.

The cross is God's balancing stick. If you're not sure that a certain teaching emphasis is properly balanced, examine it through the lens of the cross. The cross is the surest antidote to theological weirdness. It is time to gaze with new wonder at the passion of Christ's cross.

In a recent magazine column Mike Bickle writes, "I believe the most significant item on God's prophetic agenda is the release of a new passionate affection for Jesus." He goes on to say, "One of the most precise prophetic promises God ever gave me is that He would give a great gift to the church in the '90s: leaders who are passionate for Jesus." Any discerning leader reading those words responds soberly because he realizes the pathway to that caliber of leadership includes a season in God's fiery crucible.

A Passion To Be Like Him

In our church we sing a song that declares, "I want to be more like You." You should see how dispassionately some people can sing that song. While glancing at their watch, while yawning at the window, while checking out their nails, they intone, "I want to be more like You." Little wonder that Costa Deir says we do the most lying when we're singing our songs.

How strong is your yearning to be like Him? Is it enough to drive you into His presence? Because the more you're with Him, and the better you get to know Him, the more you become like Him. "...but we know that when He is revealed, we shall be like Him, for we shall see Him as He is" (1 John 3:2).

Psalm 115:8 contains the principle that we become like

that which we worship. In the example of that verse, idola-
ters become like the dead idols they worship. The inverse
holds true for those who worship the living God. The more
time you spend in His word and in His face, the more like
Him you will become.

A Passion For His House

I think the #1 disease of American Christianity is apathy.
Literally, the word means "no passion." If we do manage
to get ourselves to church on a given weekend, we arrive
in such a condition as to raise a controversy whether our
bodies comprise animate or inanimate matter.

Many a worship leader has been tempted to declare
"Code Blue" when looking over the congregation. Somebody needs to write a book on how to do CPR on a worship
service. God's people are a far cry from their Lord Jesus,
of whom it was said, "Zeal for Your house consumes Me."

God is commissioning worship leaders and worship teams
in this hour to rise up and pull God's people out of their
apathy and spiritual slumber. He is raising up anointed
minstrels and chief musicians who understand their call to
be that of stirring up the holy passions of God's people.

God has intended that believers fuel each other's fire.
When starting up a charcoal grill, you place the briquettes
close to one another in a little pile so that heat will radiate
from briquette to briquette, until the coals are hot enough
for cooking. Spread the coals out, and the fire goes out.

I never cease to be amazed at the low priority many saints
give to their attendance of corporate worship. Somebody
said, "You don't have to go to church to be a Christian." I
can tell you who told you that — the devil (1 Timothy 4:1).
Show me the Christian who doesn't think church attendance
is necessary, and I'll show you an anemic, cold Christian
with the pall of death on his countenance. Don't tell me
you have a passion for Jesus if you don't have a passion
for His house. Sleep on, O foolish virgin. You don't know
Him, and He will declare that He doesn't know you.

2. Purity

Passion for Jesus is not enough by itself. Some people have a real passion for Jesus, but they cave in to all kinds of other passions as well. Recently the Lord spoke with such conviction to my heart that I must pursue Him in *"passion with purity."* I'm talking about *moral* purity.

Moral purity is a source of great strength. My conscience is free. I have no fear of secrets being revealed. Who you see in public is who I am in private. I'm at peace with myself and God. And Satan hates it.

The devil doesn't care how much you love Jesus if he can deceive you into moral compromise. All your red-hot zeal for Christ is rendered useless by one careless, unrestrained moment. Be alerted, dear saints, that hell is launching an all-out attack to try to lure you into moral failure and sin.

"You Owe It To Yourself"

Awhile back, when I was going through an emotional valley of depression and self-pity, I was amazed at the nature of the enemy's enticements. I'm going to be very candid in describing how the tempter came to me, because I believe this chapter is going to really minister to somebody.

It was during a real battle with depression that the voice of the enemy came to me, "Just go rent a pornographic flick." It came along with thoughts like, "What's the use of going on like this? God's not paying any attention to me. Staying pure isn't getting me anywhere. What's the difference, whether I stay pure or not? I'm going down either way. To hell with it all, why not indulge myself?"

A day or two later I was reading the Bible when the devil tempted me right from the Scriptures. I know he quoted Scripture when he tempted Jesus, but this was the first time he quoted Scripture to tempt me. I was reading Proverbs 31, and came to verse 6, "Give strong drink to him who is perishing, and wine to those who are bitter of heart." The tempter whispered clearly in my ear, "That's you. This verse is describing you. Go ahead, and get drunk — compliments of the Bible!"

It is only because of God's grace that I can gratefully say

I didn't succumb to either temptation, but I was amazed at how palpable the temptations were in a time of emotional weakness and mental turmoil.

A False Fire

Then the Lord turned my thoughts toward Isaiah 50:10-11:

> *Who among you fears the LORD? Who obeys the voice of His Servant? Who walks in darkness and has no light? Let him trust in the name of the LORD and rely upon his God. Look, all you who kindle a fire, who encircle yourselves with sparks: Walk in the light of your fire and in the sparks you have kindled — This you shall have from My hand: You shall lie down in torment.*

I knew these verses were talking about times of emotional darkness that sometimes engulf God's servants, and that the temptation was to kindle your own fire when everything seems dark. But then I saw what it meant to kindle your own fire — it means to indulge yourself in a false fire because God is withholding His light for a season. Moral sin is never so tempting as the time when you feel that God has forsaken you.

But here's the warning of the passage: in that time of darkness, if you succumb to the temptation to light a false fire of moral compromise, you will lie down in torment. I knew that if I gave in to that temptation, it would be highly destructive in my life. To use something like alcohol as a way to retreat from pain is absolutely devastating.

I am presently in a season where I am seeking God with great personal longing and yearning of soul. But the purpose of my heart is to seek Him in passion *and* in purity.

3. Perseverance

This is the final principle: we must seek God's face passionately, with purity, and with perseverance.

Perhaps you've noticed that in these days God just doesn't seem to be in a hurry. And His Spirit is constantly calling us to persevere, to be steadfast, to endure patiently, to bear up, and to wait. The New Testament word "perseverance" describes the capacity to bear up under difficult circumstances, not with a passive complacency, but with a hopeful fortitude that actively resists weariness and defeat.

The Spirit is saying much today about waiting on the Lord. When seed is sown in shallow soil it springs up quickly. When seed is placed in good soil, you've got to wait for it to come up. When God plants deeply in your life, you'll have to learn to wait.

Wait A Minute

I have five things to say about waiting.

First statement: I hate it.

I hate waiting in grocery lines or at the doctor's office, I hate sitting at red lights, I don't like to wait while the car oil is being changed, and I really don't like to wait on the first hole when I've reserved a tee-off time.

Waiting kills me.

Waiting on the Lord kills me.

Wait a minute. Now I'm seeing something. That's what He's trying to do. He's taking so long because He wants me to die to myself.

Second statement: Waiting is an act of humility.

Everybody loves the grace that God gives to the humble, but who enjoys the pathway to humility? One of God's foremost ways to cultivating humility in us is "waiting." Waiting is humbling because it is a posture of dependence. "Father, I don't know what to do right now, so I'm waiting until You speak." Some of us don't walk in God's will because we're too busy to wait for it to be revealed.

Expectation

Third statement: Waiting is an act of faith.

The other day I saw a man waiting at a bus stop, and I was amazed at how long he stood there. He wasn't calling 911 or tapping his watch, he was just standing and waiting, expectantly. He was waiting because he knew the bus was coming.

When you wait on God, it's because you believe that He

will come to you. Derek Prince has said that if you're not prepared to give time, you can't expect to hear from God. He says God wants the kind of open-ended time that says, "I'm here until I hear from You, no matter how long it takes."

> *Therefore the Lord will wait, that He may be gracious to you; and therefore He will be exalted, that He may have mercy on you. For the Lord is a God of justice. Blessed are all those who wait for Him.* (Isaiah 30:18)

> *For they shall not be ashamed who wait for Me.* (Isaiah 49:23)

Fourth statement: Waiting puts us in a receiving posture.

It's possible to try to get things from God the wrong way. Bob Mumford has so capably articulated that God wants us to *receive* what He's giving, instead of trying to *take* what He's not giving. That was the mistake Adam and Eve made; they began to take what God wasn't giving instead of receiving what He offered.

My wife, Marci, illustrated it this way: When the table is spread for dinner, everything on that table belongs to our children. But if they try to pick off some pickles before it's mealtime, their sticky fingers will earn a reprimand. Why? Because they are trying to take rather than waiting to receive what is theirs.

Have you ever taken notice of how they were waiting in the upper room when the Holy Spirit fell in the second chapter of Acts? The Bible says they were just sitting there. They weren't trying to work something up. Peter wasn't trying to get everybody to dance, and shout, and cry. They were just sitting and waiting. And in the fullness of time, God blasted through the place. When God chooses to visit you, you don't have to worry about working something up; you'll know you've been visited. You've got to believe that God can show up without your help.

God's Timing

My final statement on waiting is this: There is only one way to come to an understanding of the timing of the Lord, and that is through waiting.

You don't have to be long with the Lord before you're mystified by His timing. He seems to be late all the time. He takes forever to do something that you know He could do in a moment. At other times He does in a moment what you were expecting would take years. God's sense of timing, like all His ways, is vastly different from ours.

Jesus touched on this disparity on an occasion when His brothers were prodding Him to depart immediately for Jerusalem for the Feast of Tabernacles. Jesus said to His brothers, "My time has not yet come, but your time is always ready" (John 7:6).

The Holy Spirit showed me how that statement describes me. My time is always now. If I'm in financial straits, then I want that need met *now*. If I see an opportunity, I want the door to open *now*. If I'm sick, I want to be healed *now*. I'm always ready. My flesh is absolutely incapable of tuning in to God's sense of timing.

King Saul was scandalized, on one occasion, by God's timing. Samuel had promised to come within a certain time frame in order to offer up the sacrifice and bless Saul's army as they went to battle. Saul watched while Samuel's estimated time of arrival came and went. In the meantime, warriors were leaving in droves and returning home because of the indecision and fear in Saul's camp. Saul knew full well that you don't win wars without warriors, so he made a snap decision and proceeded ahead himself with offering up the sacrifice. While he was doing so, Samuel showed up and rebuked him. Saul's impatience on that occasion cost him the kingdom. Saul learned nothing about God's timing because he was unwilling to wait.

The true test of waiting happens in moments of crisis. When it's past midnight, and God is obviously too late, will you take matters into your own hands? If you'll wait, you'll gain an opportunity to learn more about God's ways. It is one of the least-known secrets of spiritual leadership, that God uses leaders who have learned to wait on Him.

One of the greatest statements in all of Scripture on waiting is found in Isaiah 40:31, "But those who wait on the Lord shall renew their strength." The context of that verse holds important instruction concerning waiting. Look back at verse 27: "Why do you say, O Jacob, and speak, O Israel: 'My way is hidden from the Lord, and my just claim is passed over by my God'?" There are times when we have a "just claim" before God, a clear scriptural promise that is rightfully ours as a child of God, but which has not yet been fulfilled in our lives. At such a time it's easy to look at God and say, "But God, you promised! I'm not claiming this promise improperly, I'm claiming it as my rightful inheritance!" When the answer tarries, it's so easy to complain that "my just claim is passed over by my God." But it is particularly in those times of unfulfilled promises that we need to wait on Him.

I want to close by quoting a promise of God for those who wait. It occurs in the context of the great statement in Isaiah 40:31, "But those who wait on the Lord shall renew their strength." I would like you to hear the words that follow nine verses later as still applying to the one who waits on the Lord. To all you wait-ers the Lord says, "You are My servant, I have chosen you and have not cast you away: Fear not, for I am with you; be not dismayed, for I am your God. I will strengthen you, yes, I will help you, I will uphold you with My righteous right hand" (Isaiah 41:9-10).

Seek His face passionately, guard your purity, and persevere until He comes to you.

CHAPTER THREE

The Pruning Process

John 15:1 *I am the true vine, and My Father is the vinedresser. 2 Every branch in Me that does not bear fruit He takes away; and every branch that bears fruit He prunes, that it may bear more fruit. 3 You are already clean because of the word which I have spoken to you. 4 Abide in Me, and I in you. As the branch cannot bear fruit of itself, unless it abides in the vine, neither can you, unless you abide in Me. 5 I am the vine, you are the branches. He who abides in Me, and I in him, bears much fruit; for without Me you can do nothing. 6 If anyone does not abide in Me, he is cast out as a branch and is withered; and they gather them and throw them into the fire, and they are burned. 7 If you abide in Me, and My words abide in you, you will ask what you desire, and it shall be done for you. 8 By this My Father is glorified, that you bear much fruit; so you will be My disciples.*

Jesus makes one thing very clear in this passage: God's intention for His people is fruitfulness. Jesus' foremost concern is not your personal happiness or comfort. His primary concern is that you be fruitful.

This fruitfulness is virtually guaranteed to true branches. Hear Jesus saying, "As you're joined to Me, as the life-giving sap of the vine flows into you, I promise that you will be fruitful." He expects "fruit" (v.2), "more fruit" (v.2), even "much fruit" (v.5) from His branches.

What Is Fruit?

What is this "fruit" that Jesus desires to cultivate in us? The most complete answer is found in Galatians 5:22-23, "But the fruit of the Spirit is love, joy, peace, longsuffering, kindness, goodness, faithfulness, gentleness, self-control. Against such there is no law." The fruit God desires to see in our lives is the personal qualities of Jesus Himself flowing out from within us.

Whereas the "gifts of the Spirit" correspond to the works of Christ, the "fruit of the Spirit" are the virtues of Christ. When the qualities of Christ become increasingly evident in our lives then we are being fruitful. "For if you possess these qualities in *increasing measure,* they will keep you from being ineffective and unproductive in your knowledge of our Lord Jesus Christ" (2 Peter 1:8, NIV).

If we manifest the genuine love of Christ, we will unavoidably touch people's lives. If we display the unspeakable joy of Jesus, our lives will spread a contagion that will inevitably infect others with that same joy. The life that showcases the virtues of Jesus will most certainly impact the world in a profoundly fruitful way.

It's A Process

Notice that Jesus doesn't say we "produce" fruit. He says we "bear" fruit. God produces the fruit in us — He does all the work. All we do is stay connected to the vine. Sometimes God does His greatest work in us when we're unaware of it, because when we truly learn to abide in Him we're not hindering the life-flow of the vine with our own human effort.

Fruit must be developed. Many times I've wished there were an easier way to get fruit. If only we could just lay hands on each other, and speak self-control into each other's lives. "Instant fruit." A great American idea, but it just doesn't happen that way in the Kingdom. It takes time to grow fruit.

Viticulture (the cultivation of grapes) is very hard work. Grape vines require constant, strenuous care. And there are many forces at work to inhibit fruitbearing, such as insects, weather, disease, foraging animals, soil depletion, etc.

The Christian also faces many enemies of fruitfulness:

Satan, persecution, the cares of this world, sin, and the flesh. So the Lord works diligently with us to make us more fruitful. I want to focus here on just one process God employs to produce greater fruitfulness in His people.

The Pruning Process

Look at verse two of our text: "Every branch in Me that does not bear fruit He takes away; and every branch that bears fruit He prunes, that it may bear more fruit." God prunes to redirect and channel growth in order that He might garner a greater harvest.

In a typical season a vine will produce from forty to sixty canes. If all those canes are left on the vine and allowed to produce the following year, the vine will not be able to support them. The fruit will fall off prematurely, or it will be small and sour — in a word, useless. So the vinedresser will prune the fifty-some canes back to just five. Dead branches are removed, and living branches are trimmed back.

Too Busy

I have discovered that a lush plant is not necessarily a fruitful plant. This was demonstrated clearly for me in our garden last year. I always plant a number of tomato plants each year, and use wire cages to support them as they grow. One plant in particular grabbed my attention last year. You should have seen this tomato plant. It was greener than the others, it grew taller than all the rest; in fact, the branches grew over the wire cage and leaned over almost all the way back down to the ground. It had a number of blossoms on it, and it promised to be the healthiest plant in the entire garden. Can you guess how many tomatoes I gleaned from that plant last year? Not a one!

You should have seen the ugly plant next to it. It was yellowing with some kind of disease, and its branches were few. But you guessed it — it produced a number of large, juicy tomatoes. With which plant, in the final analysis, do you suppose this gardener was most pleased? Even though the other plant was tall and green and verdant, I was disappointed in it because it produced no fruit.

The Lord was teaching me something: Just because there's lots of activity doesn't mean there's lots of fruit. Let me tell you what happens in a local church. As a ministry grows, it proliferates branches. We add programs. We seldom cut back, but just keep on adding. And my, are we busy. Finally, God has to come to us in a forceful way and say, "It's time to cut back and slow down."

The same kind of thing happens with individuals. When God blesses someone's ministry, he or she begins to become fruitful. As we become fruitful, the demands on us increase. "Sister, we've seen such an anointing in this area of your ministry, so we were wondering, would you be willing to come speak at our conference?" "Brother, we've been so blessed by the way God has used you in that area, we were wondering if you'd be willing to bring your anointed leadership to help us over here in this other area?" It's exciting to watch the Lord opening up opportunities. You feel needed, and useful. And fruitful.

Then the Lord gently whispers, "Could you spend some extra time with Me today?" My heart says, "Oh yes, Lord; just let me finish this project right here, and I'll be right with you..." So in His mercy God comes to us and cuts away.

Pain

Pruning hurts. Major league pain. "God, you're killing me!" God says, "Yup."

I'm told that the way a veteran gardener prunes is really shocking to the novice. Your first response in watching the pruner would be to cry out, "Stop! You're killing the thing! At that rate you're not going to get any fruit next year at all. What did that poor plant ever do to you?"

A pruned vine looks butchered. One encyclopedia described pruning as "organized destruction." You look at that dear saint, lift your eyes to heaven, and implore, "Ease up, God. Enough already!"

Some of us are unprepared, in times of seering pain, to consider the possibility that this might be the loving hand of the Father, pruning His branch as He sees fit.

Training

I would like to substitute the word "pruning" for "chastening" as I quote Hebrews 12:11: "Now no [pruning] seems to be joyful for the present, but painful; nevertheless, afterward it yields the peaceable fruit of righteousness to those who have been trained by it." Even though pruning is painful, this verse declares, "afterward... fruit!" A harvest is promised to those who are trained by the pruning process.

Some things can be taught, but some things must be trained. Sometimes God wants to do something in us that cannot be imparted simply by giving us a principle or spiritual truth to learn. Some things in God must be walked through. If it was a lesson you were to learn, He would have taught you, you would have learned it, you would have begun to live out that word, and it would be done. But this time it's an experience you've got to be trained by.

Is there anyone honest enough to admit you like to be in charge of your personal growth? "Teach me, Lord, and I'll change." But pruning isn't something we can do for ourselves. God must do the pruning.

The Alternative

And yet, as painful as pruning is, the alternative is even more frightening. The Bible talks about it in Isaiah, chapter five.

In the book of Isaiah God refers to His people as a vineyard. God says He did everything He possibly could to make the people of Israel a fertile vineyard. "I put you on a fertile hill, and cultivated you carefully, but all you produced was wild grapes." I want you to consider the judgment God handed down against His rebellious people. "Therefore," God said, "I'm not going to prune you anymore." (See Isaiah 5:6.) When God no longer prunes, it is a sign of judgment. The consequence is desolation.

"Lord, even though it hurts, don't stop pruning me."

The Winter Season

God always prunes at the right time — during the winter season. The sap has slowed, and the vine is at rest. This is when pruning does the least amount of damage. Where the canes are cut off, open wounds remain. During winter, the diseases and pests that would otherwise infect the branch are also dormant.

For a vine to be fruitful, it must have a dormant season. The rigors of winter naturally induce dormancy in the vines. Interestingly enough, there's a portion of India where they grow grapes, but where they have no real winter. It never gets cold enough to induce the plants to rest. So guess what the farmers do? After the harvest they induce dormancy artificially. They strip off all the leaves, cut back the roots, and deprive the vine of water. This has the same shocking effect as the cold of winter, and the vine shuts down.

When God is pruning, allow me to offer some simple counsel. It's time to rest. If you don't slow down, you're headed for burnout.

During a season of abundant harvest, there is tremendous activity. There are many opportunities for ministry, and it's go, go, go. The time of harvest is the most strenuous work of the year. But take a cue. When the pruning starts, it's time to rest.

Fruitful Branches Get Pruned

Please underscore that statement. Fruitful branches get pruned. If I were Jesus, I would have worded John 15:2 a little differently. I would have said, "Every branch that bears no fruit gets pruned. And every branch that bears fruit gets encouraged, loved, pampered, coddled, and caressed." But Jesus said it is the fruitful branches who get pruned. And the unfruitful branches get tossed.

We need to understand the nature of pruning. Pruning doesn't mean simply removing what is bad. It means cutting away the good and even the better so that we might enjoy the *best*.

You're going along, serving the Lord, being fruitful, fulfilling your call, and WHAM!

"What was *that*??"

"Where did *that* come from?"

Your head starts to spin. You feel dizzy all over. Suddenly you can't tell up from down, left from right. You lose all sense of spiritual orientation. All you can see is pain, and you have no idea why.

The first sign that you've been pruned is this: God stops talking to you. As frantically as you might beseech heaven, heaven is not talking to you right now.

What's Going On?

When I don't understand something, my first response is to ask God. When I don't get an answer, my next instinct is to analyze.

When I lost my voice, the analytical side of my brain sprang to life. "God, what did I do wrong?" I looked at the circumstances surrounding my vocal injury, and tried to figure out if I had missed God somehow. Had I gotten ahead of Him? Had I wandered from the center of His purposes? My sincerest efforts to evaluate my service before God turned up nothing.

So I decided to repent. How many know it never hurts to repent? I couldn't think of any overt sin in my life, but I started to repent anyways. I repented of pride, of personal ambition, of lustful thoughts. I began to take suggestions, "Is there anything you can think of that I could repent of?" I repented of things I'd never done. When you're hurting bad enough, you're happy to repent. Anything to stop the pain.

Still no change.

"Ah," I thought next, "I know what's going on here. This is a spiritual attack." I asked my church to pray, I got people around the nation praying for me. The only problem was, I couldn't find a militant bone in my body. Just the thought of doing spiritual warfare left me feeling lifeless. If this was a demonic attack, I had no energy to do anything about it.

I'm describing my personal experience to you because when we've been pruned it's human nature to try to analyze what's happening.

Let me tell you what you did wrong, pruned one. You were *being fruitful*. God looked down upon you lovingly from heaven and said, "Good job!" K-THUNK!

Helping God Out

Allow me to make another suggestion. When God's pruning, relax the introspection. I wish it were possible to speed up the process by cooperating, but on some things God just seems to have His own timetable. It's time just now to relax and abide in Him.

Have you ever tried to advise God on how to prune? "No, God, not that. Leave that alone, Lord. If you're going to prune, God, let me suggest over here. You can prune this thing, Lord. No, Lord, I said no. Not that. I rebuke you, Satan. Get away from that thing, Lord, that thing's been fruitful. Stop, Lord. Not my prophetic ministry, Lord, prune something else. Get away from that, Lord, in Jesus' name. No, Lord, NO-O-O-O!"

K-THUNK.

"That was my arm, Lord. You just cut off my right arm."

Dayton Reynolds, the General Overseer for the fellowship of pastors of which I am a part, recently said, "The things that worked for years aren't working anymore." God is pruning back things that were once productive. Ways of ministry that were once highly effective are no longer working.

The Potter's House

You've probably read about Jeremiah's visit to the Potter's House, and the lessons God taught Jeremiah there. God said to him, "I'm the potter, you're the clay" (Jeremiah 18). One of the principles God taught Jeremiah concerning His ways with the clay vessel is this: God only allows de-struction so that He can do con-struction.

Jeremiah prophesied a great deal of judgment against the nation of Judah, and by the time they were finished with God's dealings, it would have been easy for them to say, "Whew, it's tough being on God's pottery wheel. God really does a number on you when you belong to Him." So God came with a word to His clay, the house of Judah, intending to give them understanding into His dealings with them. This word is found just a few chapters later in the book of Jeremiah. God comes to His lump of clay that has just taken the beating of its life, and declares, "For I know the thoughts that I think toward you, says the Lord, thoughts of peace and not of evil, to give you a future and a hope" (Jeremiah 29:11).

If you feel pulverized in God's hand, weary saint, then this Scripture is for you. God's purposes, although not always easy or fun, are always redemptive.

No Two Alike

Two to three years of training are necessary before one is prepared to prune grapevines, simply because each vine must be pruned uniquely. A pruner must develop an eye for each individual plant and prune it accordingly. Similarly, God prunes in each of our lives individually and uniquely.

Which is why it's dangerous to say, "God did what to you?? God's never done anything like that to me. You shouldn't be going through this, there must be something wrong somewhere."

The opposite response can be equally tempting—to share from your experience when someone else goes through the same thing. "Yeah, that happened to me once too. Let me tell you, all you need to do is..." "Here's how I overcame that challenge..."

The way you found victory probably has nothing to do with their pathway to victory, even though your circumstances may have been similar. When somebody's being pruned, most of your counsel is best kept to yourself.

When you've been pruned, I think one of the hardest aspects of that process is when you look at other branches who are in a different season in God. You look over at Sister So-And-So who is in the middle of spring or summer, and she's shouting glory. Everything is bursting forth in glorious greenery in her life, and she just radiates with the joy of the Lord.

"It's not fair, God. If I have to go through it, she does too."

To be pruned is embarrassing. Everyone else is dancing, and you feel like crying. Others are flourishing, and here you are. You don't look very spiritual at all. And when others look at you, they don't say it, but you can read their thoughts. "I wonder what she did wrong."

It feels like you're dying? Exactly.

How To Survive

I want to close this chapter by pointing out how to survive the pruning process. The key is found throughout our text in John 15, and it is in the word "abide." Abide in Christ. I'm not talking about being more disciplined with having your hour with God each morning. I'm talking about a posture of the heart that is maintained twenty-four hours a day.

We're so works oriented, we want a key, or two steps, or three principles. But Christ simply says, "Abide in Me."

When God first began to direct my attention to the pruning process, I was sharing some of my thoughts with one of my associates in ministry, Chris Wood. Chris has some background in horticulture, and he said, "Let me tell you what they do when they prune a vine."

After a branch has been pruned, he said, the increased weight of the new harvest that will come the following year will place too much strain on the branch, and the branch will snap off the vine. To avoid that, the farmer will take the branch that has been pruned, will bend it back carefully, and tie it to the vine with wire. Thus, when the increased harvest comes, the branch will be able to hold up the larger fruit without breaking. "He has stricken, but He will bind us up" (Hosea 6:1).

When Chris shared that thought with me, I realized suddenly just where I was with the Lord. I had been tied to the vine. With wire. And I couldn't move. God had hemmed me in, and all I could do was look on His face. There was nowhere else to go, nothing else to see. I had been tied to Him, face to face.

I'm still hurting. But I'm staying in His face, I'm abiding in Him. And I know that as the living sap of the vine flows into me, the life of God will eventually break forth from within into a new season of fruitfulness. He has promised, a new harvest is coming.

"Here I abide, Jesus. In Your face."

Part Two:

Seeing Jesus

CHAPTER FOUR

Hear Him

If you abide in Me, and My words abide in you, you will ask what you desire, and it shall be done for you. (John 15:7)

In February of 1994 I came to a point of personal crisis, feeling I no longer had the ability to continue in ministry because of my vocal ailment. I was feeling completely empty both emotionally and spiritually. After preaching one weekend, I came home and announced to my wife, "I'm going away on a three-week retreat to be with the Lord, then I'm coming home to resign the ministry." I wasn't simply intending to resign the pastorate, I was going to pull out of the ministry altogether. Needless to say, that didn't exactly make my wife's day. But I was desperate for the Lord to do a work in me, and if He didn't, I knew my ministry was over.

Reading The Red

The Lord gave me very clear direction for the twenty-one days from John 15:7, "If you abide in Me, and My words abide in you, you will ask what you desire, and it shall be done for you." I knew what I desired from the Lord (to be healed), and in order for that to happen I needed to abide in Him, and have His words abide in me. I felt like I had been abiding in Him, but it didn't seem like His words were abiding in me. So I felt directed of the Spirit to immerse myself in the four Gospels, giving myself entirely to the life and words of Jesus. I took His statement literally, "If *My* words abide in you," so

I directed myself to the words Jesus Himself uttered.

In my Bible all the words of Jesus are printed in red ink, so if it was in red I read it. I found red in the book of Revelation, so I read those portions. I found some red in Acts — if Jesus spoke it, I read it. I began in the Gospel of Matthew, and since I was in no rush, I enjoyed the luxury of being able to meditate in a phrase or thought for as long as I cared to. I chewed on every line, every word. Over the course of the three weeks I managed to read through the Gospels of Matthew, Mark, Luke and John three times each.

As I came to the life of Jesus I prayed, "Jesus, reveal Yourself to me. I lay aside all my preconceptions of who You are, all my theological biases, everything that I've ever assumed You to be. I'm going to read about Your life, Lord, as though it's the first time I've ever read it. And I'm asking You to show me who You really are."

For the first five days I wondered why I was there. Nothing was happening. I wasn't getting any mighty revelations. I had no visions. But around the sixth day I began to realize something was happening inside of me. The power that is in the words of Jesus was having an effect on my weary, depleted soul, and I began to be quickened in my spirit. I was waking up in the middle of the night with thoughts of Jesus erupting in my mind. I literally wept, as it was the first time in many months that the word of God had flowed inspirationally in my heart.

I want to share with you some of the things the Lord spoke to me during that retreat, while I was in His face. It will take more than one chapter to do that. But let me begin in this chapter by sharing with you the "word" that I have cherished perhaps the most.

Hardness Of Heart

You're one of the twelve disciples, and you're traveling with Jesus. It's been a long day, there are about five thousand men in the crowd besides women and children, and there's no supply of food nearby, so Jesus decides to multiply some loaves and fish for the crowd. He hands you a loaf, and you also begin to tear it in half over and over and feed a section of the crowd. Imagine it, you're watching bread and fish multiply in your own hands!

You've got to admit it, if you had actually been one of the disciples, surely that experience would have catapulted you into an incredible dimension of powerful faith. To be sure, let's see what it did for the disciples.

> *That same night Jesus came out to their boat, walking on the water. The disciples, thinking they were seeing a ghost, cried out in terror. Jesus said, "Be of good cheer! It is I; do not be afraid." Then He went up in to the boat to them, and the wind ceased. And they were greatly amazed in themselves beyond measure, and marveled. For they had not understood about the loaves, because **their heart was hardened.*** (Mark 6:51-52)

This is an important principle: Hardness of heart is not a willful, stubborn refusal to believe God. The disciples were not denying the miracle of the multiplied loaves. But even though they had watched it happen, and even though they wanted desperately to believe like Jesus did, they could not. Their hearts were hard.

Hardness of heart is a sickness that afflicts the hearts of sincere followers of Jesus Christ. We've made Jesus the Lord of our lives, but we still have hard hearts.

We're going to skip down two chapters in Mark's Gospel, to the story of the feeding of the four thousand. Imagine yourself once again as one of the disciples. If the feeding of the five thousand didn't "take" in your spirit, surely the second time around you'll become a mighty man of faith and power.

But once more, even after helping Jesus feed the four thousand, the disciples are still struggling to believe. It's after the feeding of the four thousand that Jesus has to say to them, "Is your heart still hardened?" (Mark 8:17).

Seeing the miraculous does not soften the heart or produce faith. In fact, the demonstration of the miraculous produced two opposite effects in the lives of those who witnessed it. When Jesus raised Lazarus from the dead, one group believed in Him, and another group went off to the Pharisees to blow the whistle on Jesus (see John 11:45-46). I've often thought, "If only we had more miracles happening in our churches today, more people would be getting saved." But people haven't changed. There are people who will look upon a genuine miracle of God and become more hardened than ever.

A hard heart is a heart that does not perceive or understand at a spiritual level. It describes a dulled spiritual perceptivity — spiritual blindness.

Four Kinds Of Soil

In His parable on the sower (Luke 8:5-8), Jesus describes four kinds of soil. Each soil type represents a condition of heart. The seed that is sown is the word of God. Notice that the quality of the seed is always good; it's the condition of the heart that determines the fruitfulness of the word.

The "wayside soil" (v.5) represents "the hard heart," and I will return to talk more about that in just a bit.

The "rocky soil" (v.6) represents "the shallow heart." In Palestine there are vast tracts of limestone rock, covered by a thin layer of earth. The soil that's there (perhaps two to four inches) is quite fertile, but the problem is the underlying rock. The seed will sprout and spring up quickly, but because it cannot sink its roots into the rock, it soon withers and dies.

This speaks of the person who has a very quick, enthusiastic response to the word of God. But underlying their zeal are some areas of carnality that they refuse to change or surrender. "I'm willing to serve you, Lord — just don't ask me to break up with my boyfriend." "Hey, I love Jesus, and I think He understands that I just can't quit drugs right now." "Now that I'm divorced, there's no way I'm going back to her." "I'm sure glad I have Jesus, but you know, I still need my psychiatrist." Beneath their enthusiasm is a mindset that will not change.

There are two problems with shallow soil. It doesn't retain moisture, and it doesn't allow for a root system to develop. The spiritual application is clear: When tough times hit, the shallow Christian doesn't know how to tap into the life-flow of the Holy Spirit; and because his spiritual life is too shallow, he's a goner.

The "thorny soil" (v.7) represents "the crowded heart." This thorny ground is deceptive. It has been turned over, and looks perfectly ready for seeding. But buried in this soil are the roots and seeds of weeds and thorns. Guess what always grows fastest — the good seed or the weeds? You got it. The weeds rise up vigorously and choke out the good plants.

Jesus said those thorns and weeds represent the "cares, riches, and pleasures of life" (Luke 8:14). Sometimes life is very daily. It's not as though we're on a quest to become a millionaire, we're just trying to pay the bills. But that daily fight to stay afloat financially, and even squirrel up some extra for vacations and retirement, has been the cause for many a "thorny Christian" to lose their way.

The "good soil" (v.8) represents "the fruitful heart." Christians aren't just automatically fruitful. We must be careful as to how we embrace the word of God, and allow it to germinate in our lives. That's why Jesus, after delivering this parable, warned them, "take heed how you hear" (Luke 8:18).

The Hard Heart

Now back to the "wayside soil" or "the hard heart." Every garden has a pathway between the cultivated rows, so the gardener can attend to the crop. That's what the wayside is, the pathway through the garden where people walk. That part of the soil gets trampled down and becomes very hard. Even though seed may be sown upon it, the seed can't penetrate. And even if it could, the birds come and snatch the seed away.

This is not the only passage in the Bible where birds symbolize demons. Some people sit in church, and while they're hearing the word of God being proclaimed they're having these kinds of thoughts: "I'm not sure I agree with that." "I don't think that's the only way to see it." And what these hard-hearted folks don't realize is, that while they're sitting in church demons are robbing them of the blessing of the word. I'm not talking here about the sincere believer who carefully evaluates what's being preached against what the Scriptures say, like the Bereans did in Acts 17:11. I'm talking about someone with a hard heart who doesn't even realize that demons are exploiting his hardness by stealing away what little word does land on his heart. Listen carefully, dear one. This is happening in our churches far more frequently than we care to admit.

The Lord whispered gently to my heart, "This is your problem, Bob. You have a hard heart."

Jesus is not horrified by your unbelief and hardness of heart. He knows how hard your heart is. But He wants you to see it. So often Jesus made statements to His disciples like, "Why do you have so little faith?" He didn't talk like that to berate them or beat them down. He talked like that to shake them awake to an understanding of the true condition of their heart. The first step to victory is seeing your hardness.

The Main Word

Unless your heart is softened and ready, you will not be able to receive what I am about to say. You might do well to set this book down for a couple minutes and ask the Lord to prepare your heart, because I am about to share something that has the potential to change your life.

While meditating in the Gospels, I suddenly saw what was the most important concept in the message of Jesus. The Lord revealed to me what was the most prominent word or thought in Jesus' teachings. It's the central word in the gospel. When I saw this, I realized that this was the most important word in the entire Bible.

I didn't get this from a commentary or a book. This was a revelation to my heart in the school of the Spirit.

It is very important that you grasp what the Spirit is wanting to say to you in this chapter, because if you can hear this word it will transform your orientation toward everything you do in the Kingdom of God. It has become for me something of a "master key" to moving and ministering in the Kingdom. It is through this one word that we unlock everything that Christ has made available to us in spiritual realms.

The word is simply this: "hear." "He who has ears to hear, let him hear!" (Matthew 11:15). Everything in the gospel is predicated upon truly and simply *hearing* what God is saying.

Maybe you thought "love" would be the most important word in the gospel. But when Jesus was asked which was the most important commandment, He quoted from the Old Testament in this manner, "*Hear*, O Israel, the Lord our God, the Lord is one. And you shall love the Lord your God, with all your heart, with all your soul, with all your mind, and with all your strength" (Mark 12:29-30).

Maybe you thought the right answer was "faith." But surely you've read the Scripture, "Faith comes by *hearing*."

Maybe you thought the word was "word." And yet, on many occasions Jesus asked the people why they didn't hear His words. What's the good of a word coming to you, if you can't hear it? The fullness of God's glorious purposes are spread openly before those who have ears to hear.

This truth penetrated my heart most forcefully when I read the account of the transfiguration (Mark 9:1-8). Peter and his buddies were enamored with the company Jesus was keeping — Moses and Elijah! But when the cloud hid them from view, the voice of the Father spoke authoritatively from the cloud, "This is My beloved Son. *Hear Him!*" (Mark 9:7). Moses represented the Law, and Elijah represented the Prophets. The Father was saying, "You've had the Law and the Prophets. Now you have my Son. Hear *Him!*"

But the Father's emphasis was not only on the second word; it was also on the first word — "*Hear* Him!"

Too Busy

I will tell you why you don't hear Him. You're not in His word. There, I said it.

Jesus had only one expectation of His disciples. He wasn't looking for them to be faithful, or believing, or intelligent. He chose them to follow Him for but one purpose, "that they might be with Him" (Mark 3:14). All He asked of them was that they be with Him and hear His words.

> *Now it happened as they went that He entered a certain village; and a certain woman named Martha welcomed Him into her house. And she had a sister called Mary, who also sat at Jesus' feet and heard His word. But Martha was distracted with much serving, and she approached Him and said, "Lord, do You not care that my sister has left me to serve alone? Therefore tell her to help me." And Jesus answered and said to her, "Martha, Martha, you are worried and troubled about many things. But one thing is needed, and Mary has chosen that good part, which will not be taken away from her."* (Luke 10:38-42)

What was the "one thing" that was needed, which Mary chose? It was to *hear His word.*

I realized I am a Martha. Do do do, work work work, serve serve serve. How many Martha's do we have out there, reading this right now? "Martha, Martha." "Bob, Bob." "Linda, Linda." "Jim, Jim." Oh, the biting reproof in those words. I'm too busy to hear Him.

You may not understand all you hear. You may not like everything you hear. But O the power in His words. There's not a challenge you face that isn't entirely dismantled with one living word from the mouth of God.

The Sounds of Babylon

You don't hear Him because you're hearing too many other things. Oprah Winfrey, Sally Jesse Raphael, Phil Donahue. You're licking your fingers on the delicacies of Babylon. An evening that could be spent hearing the words of Jesus is squandered before the tube. "As the World Burns." Pity the Christian who has rationalized watching soap operas. It's vulture's food.

You get in your car in the morning, and on the way to work tune into your "Contemporary Adult Rock" music station. Jiving to the jingles of Babylon. Humming the melodies of the Great Harlot. And then you cry, "Oh Lord, I want to hear You." "No you don't." Did you know that in the book of Revelation they mourn the death of the songs of Babylon?

Some Christians have got to have their daily laugh with Rush Limbaugh, that "mouth speaking great things and blasphemies" (Revelation 13:5).

Or maybe it's CNN. I watched the newscast carefully, and after it was all over I realized it was the same news I had sat through four hours earlier! We'll watch the same news clippings over and over. When Christ has given the invitation to hear Him.

You laugh at the sitcoms, you stare at the documentaries, you sit through the movies, you rent the videos. Hardhearted Christian, stop pretending that you want to hear His words. How can you claim to want to hear Him when you're doing everything possible to obliterate the sound of His voice?

The Sound Of His Voice

As you spend "soaking time" in the words of Jesus, you start to get your ear tuned to His voice. The more you tune into the timbre of His voice, the easier it becomes to recognize a different voice.

I experienced this while reading through the Gospels. I opened to the letters to the seven churches in Revelation, chapters two and three, and as I was reading the red lettering in those chapters I suddenly realized something — this is the way Jesus talks! The voice of Jesus in the Gospels was the same voice as that in the book of Revelation. And then a couple days later I was reading a commentary that said, "In this passage Jesus means to say such and such." When I read that, there rose up something from within me that cried, "No! Those are not the words of Jesus!" I had become so tuned to the sound of Jesus' voice that I was able to recognize the false.

Many of you can't hear Him because you don't even recognize the sound of His voice. And you don't recognize when a different voice comes to you. You have made decisions based on what you thought Jesus was saying to you, but you were so unfamiliar with the sound of His voice that you were duped.

So now you're allowing a romantic relationship in your life, and you've got yourself convinced that Jesus approves.

You went out and bought the nicest car you could afford, and thought that Jesus approved.

You thought He okayed the home improvement loan you took out.

You accepted that job promotion, thinking the Lord was enabling you to tithe more to the work of God, but now you barely have any time for the Kingdom.

Are you sure you know the sound of His voice?

Hearing The Preacher

Consider how nonchalantly you listen to the preaching of the word. As you sit under the feeding of your shepherd, there is no pen in your hand, you didn't even bring any paper to note what the Holy Spirit is saying to your heart, you do not lean forward with anticipation, your eyes are not fixed and focussed, your heart is hard. I will give you five reasons why your Bible is not open before you, and why you have delegated note-taking to your spouse:

1. You didn't pray for the meeting and the preacher, so you have no faith to believe that God will use him to bring a word of life to your heart [*prayerlessness*].
2. You didn't expect that the preacher would be able to lift anything from the word that you have not already heard [*arrogance*].
3. You are indifferent because you are already fat and

well fed [*barrenness*].
4. You are so arrogant as to think that you can remember one hour later that living word which God speaks to you, when in the hardness of your heart you have consistently forgotten previous words He has brought to you [*deception*].
5. You do not believe God will honor His promise to bless those who "hunger and thirst after righteousness, for they shall be filled" [*unbelief*].

Your hearing Him precedes His hearing you. God did mighty miracles through the ministry of Jesus and He heard His Son every time for one simple reason: Jesus first of all heard the Father. Just before raising Lazarus Jesus prayed, "I know that You always hear Me" (John 11:42). Oh, how I have longed to be able to utter those words to the Father! So often I question whether He is really hearing me. But I am learning that if I want to be heard, I must first of all hear Him.

His Thoughts, His Ways

"For My thoughts are not your thoughts, Nor are your ways My ways," says the Lord. "For as the heavens are higher than the earth, so are My ways higher than your ways, and My thoughts than your thoughts." (Isaiah 55:8-9)

Make this assumption from the start: If I think of it, it doesn't resemble God's thoughts. If I would do it a certain way, I can be assured that it isn't God's way, unless I first of all receive it from Him. Because His thoughts and ways are literally a universe above mine.

There is only one way to have the thoughts of God, or to walk in the ways of God, and that is by hearing Him. If I am not walking the path that He has laid out for me, I am doomed to the frustration of walking in my human effort.

I realize now that I have lived my life far too confidently. I have been bold and visionary when my thoughts and ways were vastly divergent from God's. Worship leaders need to lose their confidence in themselves. Pastors need to come to a new level of dependence upon every word that comes from God's mouth. We can no longer afford to take a solitary step apart from the voice of God.

CHAPTER FIVE

A Softened Heart

After reading the previous chapter, many of us have a fresh awareness of the hardness of our hearts. How did our hearts get that way?

Things That Harden

Very quickly, I want to point to some of the ways our hearts become hardened. When I see another believer in need, and I have the means to minister some relief to that needy believer but instead I close my hand to him or her, the Bible says that I am hardening my heart (Deuteronomy 15:7). When I hold back from a good work I know the Lord wants me to do, my heart hardens.

Sin hardens the heart (Hebrews 3:13), and does so very deceptively. When we neglect the rudimentary elements of the Christian walk (prayer, reading the Scriptures, tithing, faithfulness to God's house, etc.) we harden our hearts.

In Luke 21:34, Jesus pointed to three other things that harden our hearts: "But take heed to yourselves, lest your heart be weighed down with carousing, drunkenness, and cares of this life, and that Day come on you unexpectedly." Carousing, drunkenness, and the cares of this life weigh our hearts down, trampling down the soil of our hearts. Regarding carousing and drunkenness I will only say this: The Christian does not belong in the party life of the world. Allow yourself to dabble with the bar scene, and you're dangerously hardening your heart. The "cares of this life" are not necessarily evil or wrong things, they're just the normal everyday challenges of life. In other words, all you have to do to harden your heart is be about the normal tasks of everyday living.

If we're going to soften our hearts, we must rise above the normal, above the human, and touch the heavenly.

Two Spiritual Disciplines

Someone might ask, "Now that I see that my heart is hard, what do I do about it?" That's what this chapter is about. I want to highlight two spiritual disciplines that are designed by God to soften our hearts.

The first is fasting. As soon as you read that word, I know that some of you are inclined to move right on to the next chapter. Don't. God wants you to come to a new dimension of breakthrough in the area of fasting, and this chapter is important reading for you.

"What torturous spirit took hold of God on the sadistic day He invented fasting?" someone might ask. "What kind of Father is He anyways, that He delights to watch us deprive and starve ourselves?"

If you see fasting as a punishment or a hardship, you're missing the point altogether. Fasting is a glorious provision of God that enables the desperate soul to find a tangible way to express the great longing of his heart. Some of you have never fasted simply because you've never been desperate enough.

I don't know of a more aggressive way to seek God than in fasting. It's one of the ways the Kingdom suffers violence. Somebody says, "I'll fast if God tells me to." Then you'll never fast. Fasting isn't something you do out of obedience, it's something you do because you're desperately hungry for God. When your body cries out for food, your soul cries even louder, "Lord, my desire for food is nothing compared to my desire for You."

Fasting is an expression of grief (Joel 2:12, Daniel 10:2-3, et al). "Blessed are those who mourn." When you're mourning your spiritual condition, fast. "Lament and mourn and weep! Let your laughter be turned to mourning and your joy to gloom. Humble yourselves in the sight of the Lord, and He will lift you up" (James 4:9-10). Fasting is one of the most self-emptying, humbling things you can do, and we know God has promised grace to those who humble themselves (James 4:6).

Real Food

Never before had I fasted for so long, but I decided to fast during my three-week retreat. Not only did it make my retreat more meaningful, it also gave me fresh insight into the dynamics and benefits of fasting. I didn't fast completely, mind you, I had a meal every day: the Lord's Supper. As I took the bread each morning, my stomach growling for a complete breakfast, I would say, "Lord, *You* are my food." I cannot describe what happens inside you when you say to God with all your soul, "My necessary food is not my food. My food is the words of Jesus. My food is to do the will of God. You are my food, O Lord."

It is on a prolonged fast that these words of Jesus come alive: "Man shall not live by bread alone, but by every word that proceeds from the mouth of God" (Matthew 4:4). Fasting will give you an appetite for the food of heaven.

Overcoming Temptation

The desire for food is the most basic of all appetites. It was food that got this planet into its present mess in the first place. (Adam & Eve capitulated to the desire of their stomachs and ate what was forbidden.) When we fast, we are making a deliberate choice to defy the very appetite that produced sin in us at the beginning. Our example is the Last Adam, who in the face of the temptation to turn stones to bread, denied His stomach.

From the belly spring all the appetites or lusts or desires, which is why when you're fighting a battle with fleshly desires that fasting is such a powerful weapon. If you can deny your belly, you can deny virtually any other appetite. To the reader who has an ongoing struggle with an area of habitual sin let me ask, have you yet availed yourself of the weapon of fasting? Fasting was employed by Jesus to overcome the temptation of the adversary (see Matthew 4:1-11).

Gaining Perspective

During my three-week fast, I began to gain new perspective. Fresh perspective is promised to those who wait on Him — "they shall mount up with wings as eagles" (Isaiah 40:31). But it wasn't the kind of perspective I was asking for. I was asking God for understanding regarding His purposes in my life, and where He was leading me. Instead, He gave me perspective on the worldliness of my lifestyle. I began to see my own worldliness, and the worldliness of the church.

Much of what the Lord spoke to me in this regard centered around one tiny phrase of the gospel: "let him deny himself." This phrase is found in Matthew 16:24, "Then Jesus said to His disciples, 'If anyone desires to come after Me, let him deny himself, and take up his cross, and follow me.'" We have heard much about taking up the cross, and about following Jesus, but we have heard relatively little about denying ourselves.

Until you deny yourself, you will never see the world. Because the world denies itself nothing. The worldly person operates like this: "If I want it, and I can afford it, I get it." But to be a disciple of Jesus, you must deny yourself.

Deny your belly. Unless, of course, your belly runs your life. "For many walk, of whom I have told you often, and now tell you even weeping, that they are the enemies of the cross of Christ: whose end is destruction, whose god is their belly, and whose glory is in their shame — who set their mind on earthly things. For our citizenship is in heaven" (Philippians 3:18-20).

If there's one thing the world doesn't deny itself, it's their stomach. We are a "restaurant society." Just drive down "gastric boulevard" and look at all the eateries: McDonalds, Burger King, Wendys, Arbys, Pizza Hut, Ponderosa, Taco Bell, Perkins, Hardees, Little Caesars, Lubys, Subway, Dennys, and the list goes on and on. Food food food, eat eat eat, belly belly belly. Relax. Enjoy. The only problem being Jesus' words: "If anyone desires to come after Me, let him deny himself."

Your little luxuries and indulgences are not necessarily sinful, but they keep your heart so close to your belly that you cannot maintain perspective on the Kingdom of God.

Self-denial gets your heart out of your stomach, enabling you to regain Kingdom focus. We do not fast to impress God or move Him to action; we fast for the purpose of gaining clearer spiritual perceptivity.

Just Do It

There are different kinds of fasts. Some fast one meal a day, or for an entire day. Some drink only water, others will drink juices. The Bible records fasts that lasted for a day, for three days, for seven days, for twenty-one days, and for forty days.

American Christians have invented the most ingenious methods for taking the sting out of fasting. We think we're being spiritual when we fast from TV for a week. Or we fast from chocolate. "I'm fasting from in-between-meal snacks." Impressive.

Let me place a challenge before you. I want you to consider a multiple-day fast. Unless you have a health restriction, set aside a number of days for fasting and prayer, and water only. We all claim we want to be like Jesus, but when we look at His example of fasting for forty days most of us don't even think that portion of His life has any application to us at all.

Make a decision, get out your calendar, and schedule it in. Do it at a time when you can sanctify yourself completely to seek the Lord. Take the time off work. Pull away from social distractions. I think every believer should experience at least once the delight of a week-long fast in this fashion. If you have health restrictions (such as sugar diabetes), consult your doctor, and eat only what is absolutely necessary, with as little flavoring and preparation involved as possible. If you obey this word, dear saint, you will never regret it.

An Old Garment

Here's where I'm going with all this: Fasting is used by God to soften our hearts. We wanted our heart softened, remember? Fasting softens the heart and sensitizes the ear.

"How does fasting soften our heart?" The answer to that is found in the words of Jesus.

*"But the days will come when the bridegroom will
be taken away from them; then they will fast in those
days." 36 Then He spoke a parable to them: "No one
puts a piece from a new garment on an old one; otherwise the new makes a tear, and also the piece that was
taken out of the new does not match the old. 37 And no
one puts new wine into old wineskins; or else the new
wine will burst the wineskins and be spilled, and the
wineskins will be ruined. 38 But new wine must be put
into new wineskins, and both are preserved. 39 And no
one, having drunk old wine, immediately desires new;
for he says, 'The old is better.'"* (Luke 5:35-39)

These parables of the old garment and the old wineskin
are not explained by Jesus, and consequently many different
interpretations have been offered. But the key to understanding
these parables is by connecting them to the previous verses.
Jesus is talking about fasting, and when He comes to verse
36 He continues to address the subject of fasting.

Jesus uses two metaphors in this passage to illustrate
what fasting accomplishes in us. First of all, He talks about
a new patch being sewn onto an old garment. Jesus gave two
reasons for avoiding that kind of thing: 1) When a new piece
of cloth begins to shrink with washing, it will tear the old
garment because it is stronger; 2) It is not a precise match,
even though at one time the patterns were identical, because
the old garment has faded with time and use.

Let me explain the symbolism of this parable. The old
garment represents you; the new patch represents what
God wants to do in you. Jesus was saying that the only way
we old garments can accept the new thing God wants to do
among us is by being made new ourselves, being restored to
our original condition.

"What does all this have to do with fasting?" Fasting (and
prayer) is the means God uses to take an old, faded saint, and
revitalize and restore him to his first love. As we are made
new ourselves through fasting, the new patch of what God
wants to do can be sewn into our lives.

An Old Wineskin

Jesus makes the same point again, this time using the analogy of a wineskin. A wineskin is made from the hide of an animal (such as a goat). It is sewn into the shape of a pouch, and then used to process wine.

When new wine is put into a new wineskin, the enzymes and chemical reactions that cause the wine to become fully aged go to work. The changes that take place within the wine are considerable, and require the wineskin to flex and expand accordingly. But the time comes when the wine is properly aged, and the changes stop. At that point, the wineskin will harden into a certain shape and size.

If you try to put new wine into that old, hardened wineskin, the old wineskin will not be able to flex and expand with all the new changes, and instead of stretching it will burst. Thus, wineskin and new wine are both ruined.

Here's the symbolism: The new wine represents the fresh thrust of the Holy Spirit, and the old wineskin represents the Church with its present structures, systems, modes of operation, and ways of thinking. The present Church systems cannot handle the new wine of the Holy Spirit. The stretch is simply too much.

This explains why revivals have split churches and literally divided denominations. If a wineskin is not prepared, it will not be able to handle the new move of the Spirit.

My heart cries, "Lord, I know I'm hardhearted. I know I resist You. But I don't want to miss what You're doing in the earth in this hour. What can I do to soften my heart?" The Lord's answer is in this parable — through fasting. Fasting and prayer softens the heart.

Your flesh will resist this message. Notice that Jesus went on to say in verse 39 that old wineskins always prefer the old wine. They are not only incapable of receiving the new wine, they're not even interested in it. But there are those within whom God has placed a thirst for new wine. Get in His face, seek Him desperately in fasting and prayer, and He will pour some of the new wine into you.

Fasting And Spiritual Warfare

Before I move on to the second thing that softens our hearts, I want to touch very briefly on one thing related to fasting that disturbs me greatly. It regards the decision of many contemporary translators to relegate to the margin or footnotes a central teaching of Jesus' on fasting. In Matthew 17:21, Jesus instructed His disciples in a powerful ingredient to gaining victory over demonic powers — fasting and prayer. But for textual reasons, the NIV omits the verse entirely and makes it a footnote at the bottom of the page; the RSV does the same thing; the NAS also omits the verse, adding it in a marginal note. (I mention those translations only because they are among the most popular, but some others do the same thing.)

In the parallel verse of Mark 9:29, these translations will say that demons come out only by prayer, but the words "and fasting" are again omitted, and stuck in the margin or footnotes. In other words, if you use one of these translations and are not inclined to reading the margin notes or footnotes, you will never encounter the message that "prayer and fasting" plays a critical role in exerting authority over demonic powers. And even if you do read the footnotes, let me ask an honest question: Who really gives a lot of credence to a footnote anyways?

A crucial kingdom principle has been assigned to the footnotes of our Bibles. Now who do you think might be the inspiration behind the clever disguising of such a powerful teaching of our Lord on spiritual warfare?

I changed the pew Bible in our church to the New King James Version, and now preach from that translation, because I want my flock to encounter those words of Christ when they read through the Scriptures.

You might argue that those translations have a viable textual basis for omitting certain words and verses, and my criticism might sound naive and uninformed and narrow to some. But if you knew the sound of Jesus' voice, when you read His directive to "prayer and fasting" you too would recognize them as the true words of Jesus.

The Hammer

There is one more thing that softens the heart, and that is the word of God. "'Is not My word like a fire?' says the Lord, 'And like a hammer that breaks the rock in pieces?'" (Jeremiah 23:29). God's word is likened unto a hammer that can shatter even rock into pieces. The hammer of God's word, when applied to the rock-hard areas of my heart, will bring me to a place of brokenness and softness before Him.

As I spent time in the words of Jesus, it seemed to me as though the Lord grabbed me with His tongs, stuck me in the fire, pulled me out, put me down on His anvil, and began to pound me straight with the hammer of His word. God was straightening out some of my misplaced, skewed ideas.

I began to see Jesus in a new way. The Jesus I was seeing was so gripping that I asked, "Where have I been, Lord? Why have I not seen You like this before?"

One of the things the Lord pounded straight in my life was the emphasis in my preaching on the Epistles, to the neglect of the Gospels. The Lord helped me to realize that most of my sermons were rooted in the Epistles, and I had actually overlooked, to a significant degree, the message of the Gospels in my pulpit ministry. I asked the Lord, "How did this happen?" and He revealed to me some misconceptions I had about Jesus Himself. These misconceptions had in turn caused me to gloss a little too quickly over the Gospels in my reading and studying. Let me summarize quickly the two major misconceptions I had about Jesus Christ.

Over-Exaggeration

I had adopted the idea that Jesus used hyperbole as a teaching tool. Hyperbole is a way of exaggerating and overstating the case in order to make a point. "I've told you a million times…" is a form of hyperbole. In literature, hyperbole is a completely valid and acceptable art form. A hyperbole is not a lie when it is understood that one is purposefully exaggerating for the sake of emphasis. But I realized through the Holy Spirit's help that I had avoided the teachings of Jesus to a certain extent because I grew tired of trying to figure out what was exaggeration and what was not.

Some of Jesus' statements seemed to me to be exagger-
ated to make a point. Statements like the following caused
me to think Jesus used hyperbole: "It is easier for a camel to
go through the eye of a needle than for a rich man to enter
the kingdom of God" (Luke 18:25); "If anyone comes to Me
and does not hate his father and mother, wife and children,
brothers and sisters, yes, and his own life also, he cannot be
My disciple" (Luke 14:26). Hate father and mother? Surely
not! Surely that's an overstatement!

It was tempting to teach like this: "What Jesus is trying to
say here is..." As though I could do a better job than Jesus of
saying what was in His mind. Listen, my friend, Jesus didn't
try to say anything. He said it! Jesus had the brainpower to
say exactly what He meant, and to mean exactly what He
said. I had to settle it clearly in my mind: Jesus never used
hyperbole. In fact, over and again Jesus made emphatic
statements like, "Assuredly I say to you..." "Verily, verily..."
He did His utmost to try to get it through to His hearers, "I'm
not inflating this in the least, I don't know how to make it
any clearer, I'm saying it exactly the way it is!" Jesus cut it
straight.

Incomplete Grace

Here's another misconception I had about Jesus that the
Lord pounded straight in my mind through the hammer of
His word: I had the idea that Jesus didn't teach in the fullness of grace during His earthly ministry because Calvary
had not yet happened. I don't remember reading that idea
in a book, nor was I taught that at Bible College. I had never
taught that from the pulpit. In fact, if you had accused me
of thinking that, I would have denied it. But the Holy Spirit
revealed to me that in fact that was a subconscious mindset
that caused me to gloss over the life and message of Jesus.

I think I came to that mindset because some of Jesus'
teachings seemed so hard to me, they seemed to smack more
of "law" than "grace." I conceived of Jesus as straddling the
Testaments, as though he had one foot in the Old Covenant
and one in the New. I imagined Jesus thinking, "My, I wish
I could tell you folks more about the fullness of grace, but
you just wouldn't understand yet because you don't know

anything about what I'm going to accomplish at Calvary."

God straightened me out with one swift reminder that Jesus came "*full* of grace and truth" (John 1:14). We must have it clearly established in our hearts that every word and teaching of Jesus was a full expression of God's grace to man.

Our problem is, we have a convoluted concept of grace. We have come to define grace as "the tolerance of God that allows us to live with one foot in the church and one foot in the world." That's not grace, that's foolishness. Such a person is neither hot nor cold, and Jesus said "I will vomit you out of My mouth" (Revelation 3:16).

Grace is the kindness of God toward mankind, evidenced by sending His Son to die for us and redeem us to Himself, that we might be lifted from the filth of this world and live in the glory of His righteousness. God forbid that we should exploit His grace in order to return to the filth from which we have been redeemed.

The Full Gospel

Yes, Jesus came full of grace. He preached the full gospel. I used to think that the gospel age was officially inaugurated on the Day of Pentecost (Acts 2), and therefore the complete gospel message was not to be found until the Book of Acts and the Epistles. But the Lord showed me differently from Luke 16:16, "The law and the prophets were until John. Since that time the kingdom of God has been preached." Jesus declared that the gospel age began with John the Baptist. That is why he was such a powerful prophet, although "he who is least in the kingdom of heaven is greater than he [John]" (Matthew 11:11).

The Lord hammered this truth into my heart: Jesus taught the full gospel! The gospel is in the Gospels.

I recount how the Lord has hammered me straight with His word because I want to encourage you to spend time in His word. His word will soften your heart, and straighten out your misconceptions. He will reorient you, as He did me, to a renewed preoccupation with the face of Jesus.

CHAPTER SIX

In Hollywood's Face

T his chapter is about TV, and you already know what's coming. Some of you are so thrilled you probably turned to this chapter first. Others don't even want to read another TV-bashing article. But don't set the book down now — after all, what else is there to do? Watch TV?

The Narrow Gate

"Strive to enter through the narrow gate, for many, I say to you, will seek to enter and will not be able" (Luke 13:24).

Some of you reading this book will end up in the eternal fire of hell. You say, "Not me, I'm a Christian." Yes, you. For "many...will seek to enter and will not be able." Friends, I cannot remember being so shaken by any word of Scripture in a long time.

Jesus is talking about Christians in this verse. There are many people sitting in our churches who want to be Christians, and who want badly to go to heaven. But Jesus said they will not be able. O pastor, tremble and weep for your flock. They just can't get Sodom out of their heart.

Imagine a very narrow passageway. You wish to go through, but find that you must turn sideways and pull in your tummy in order to move through the narrow opening. Can you see yourself? This is you, trying to enter heaven.

Now notice the things in your arms that you're trying to take with you: golf clubs, skis, fishing rod, rifle, exercise bicycle, bowling ball, and your TV & VCR. Does the image seem ridiculous to you? It is to God too. You want to get into heaven, but you love the world and the things of the world.

There's only one way to get to heaven, and that is to strive to enter. Make it the focus of your best passions and energies to enter the narrow gate.

Deny the curiosity of your flesh to tour hell on your way to heaven. Should you decide to take a sleigh ride past hell, the closer you get the harder it is to hold on. Some of you will fall right off your slippery sled as you careen past hell. You can't smell like hell and still get to heaven.

"But I'm trusting in God's grace." The grace of God will keep you only as you strive to enter the narrow gate. Make it your foremost occupation. Fix your gaze upon that narrow gate and strive to enter with all your heart and soul and body.

A Poem

I received this verse one day while in the Spirit. It applies not only to TV, but to any worldly distraction.

You watch TV instead of praying because you do not hunger and thirst after righteousness.

You watch TV instead of praying because you are fat and well fed.

You watch TV instead of praying because you like the melodies of Babylon.

You watch TV instead of praying because your eyes are dark and your heart is cold.

You watch TV instead of praying because you have a religion that is talk but has no power.

You watch TV instead of praying because you enjoy food offered up to idols.

You watch TV instead of praying because you do not understand the lateness of the hour.

You watch TV instead of praying because you have come to justify your indulgence of the flesh.

You watch TV instead of praying because you have fallen asleep while the bridegroom tarries.

Therefore, in My mercy says the Lord, I will come to you and unsettle you and make you lean and hungry and thirsty.

Let me explain the line, "You watch TV instead of praying because you enjoy food offered up to idols." The world practices and portrays its idolatry on TV. You would never do the things they do on TV, because you don't serve their idols. But when you watch them do it, you are eating the food they offer to their idols.

Applause Applause

"Woe to you who laugh now, for you shall mourn and weep" (Luke 6:25). We live in a laughter-crazed society. Turn on the TV and hear the laughter. Sitcoms. Talk shows. Late night hosts. Comedies get some of the highest ratings because Americans are dying to laugh. Never in the history of our planet have so many tormented people laughed so much.

Hear the judgment of Jesus against the TV industry: "Woe to you who laugh now." The world is laughing when it should be wailing. Worldly Christian, why do you laugh so?

"Blessed are you who weep now, for you shall laugh" (Luke 6:21). Ah, the blessing of the Lord is upon those who weep. I will tell you what to mourn: Mourn the things you cannot change. Will you mourn your worldliness? Will you weep over the hardness of your heart? Will you lament the lostness of those around you? Will you mourn our national plight? Jesus is saying, "If you're hurting, cry; if you're unhappy with your life, weep; if you're dissatisfied with your life, be sorrowful." You position yourself for blessing.

Don't confuse mourning with morbidity, as though it were a dark oppressive cloud. Mourning is not depression; mourning is the gift of God that enables your soul to express its longings in times of distress.

But we don't like to weep. We want to rejoice. I'm afraid that we've equipped the body of Christ to dance and celebrate, but we have not equipped the church of the '90s to mourn. The Psalms are chock-full of songs of mourning, and our songlists are glaringly bare of them. We have judged those who mourn as though they were doing something wrong. If God shows you the true condition of today's Laodicean church, you'll mourn!

Offenses

> *Then He said to the disciples, "It is impossible that*
> *no offenses should come, but woe to him through whom*
> *they do come! It would be better for him if a millstone*
> *were hung around his neck, and he were thrown into*
> *the sea, than that he should offend one of these little*
> *ones." (Luke 17:1-2)*

Our entertainment industry is under a curse of God
Almighty. Jesus pronounced a curse upon those who are
responsible for causing one of His little ones to stumble, and
how many children are being polluted and prepared for hell
by our entertainment industry! Videos introducing children to
pornography are throwing them into a promiscuous life-style
at early ages. MTV is inculcating rebellion. Pray for the actors
and filmmakers, for they will receive the greater condemnation.
Pray for the owners and workers of video arcades, for they will
receive the greater condemnation. Pray for the parents who
allow HBO and Showtime and Cinemax into their homes, to
defile both themselves and their children.

Pray for yourselves, and take heed to yourselves. For you
have the affections of the world in your flesh. And you yearn
to sit and stare and watch the fruit of corruption. Brothers
and sisters, we need to watch TV and rent videos in the fear
of God! Because many times, even when there is no vulgar
language, no sex, no violence, there is still many times the
immoral self-centeredness of the world on display. An evening
that could be spent hearing the words of Jesus is frittered
and wasted away. Are you honest in saying you want to hear
the words of Jesus? "All the vain things that charm me most,
I sacrifice them to His blood."

Gaining Perspective

Not all TV programs pollute. I am not saying it is sinful,
without exception, for a Christian to watch TV. We have had
a TV in our home most of our marriage, although at present
we have sold the TV and VCR in order to gain some spiritual
perspective. We have labored to control our TV viewing, although we've often failed. But there is something at risk here

that is of more significance than the potential for defilement, and it is this — the lost opportunities for communing with the Father.

We come home from work and feel tired and defiled by the world. So what do we do? Collapse in front of the TV! That's like jumping from the pigpen into the dunghill. We squander time that could have been spent washing in the water of the word, being renewed in the Spirit, hearing His voice, and exchanging love.

"If you abide in Me, and My words abide in you, you will ask what you desire, and it shall be done for you" (John 15:7). As long as you abide in the world, you cannot hear the words of God.

"And he who loves Me will be loved by My Father, and I will love him and manifest Myself to him" (John 14:21). Isn't that what you want? For Jesus to manifest Himself to you? Then turn off the TV, and open His word.

And I've got to say something about the commercials. The tentacles of the Beast reach out to entwine you from the commercials. They are forever appealing to the covetousness of your heart. They feed your greed. Their covetousness makes money off your covetousness.

John The Baptist

John The Baptist was a strange guy. He didn't do things normal people do. "Now John was clothed with camel's hair and with a leather belt around his waist, and he ate locusts and wild honey" (Mark 1:6).

There is smoother material than camel's hair. Why not wear wool, John? What's wrong with cotton?

And there are nicer, healthier foods than locusts and wild honey. Can't you imagine someone trying to invite John the Baptist over for a meal?

"John, please come have dinner with us."

"What are you having?"

"Bread and fish."

"No, I can't come."

"Why not?"

"I don't eat fish."

"You don't eat fish? Why not, John? Is there something

wrong with fish?"

"Nothing wrong with fish."

"Well, are you afraid of offending someone if you eat fish? Why don't you eat fish?"

"I just don't eat fish."

Folks, that's weird. Even eccentric. There's nothing wrong with eating fish, there's no controversy over eating fish, but John won't eat fish.

John the Baptist ate and dressed as he did because he knew that in order to have spiritual perception, one must distance himself from the sumptuous fare and everyday amenities of ordinary life. He understood that self-denial was necessary if he was to have clear Kingdom vision. It was because of his separation from the world that he was one day able to have the prophetic clarity to point his finger and declare, "Behold the Lamb of God who takes away the sins of the world!"

That kind of prophetic edge doesn't just happen. It comes with a price tag that few are willing to pay. "Then Jesus said to His disciples, 'If anyone desires to come after Me, *let him deny himself,* and take up his cross, and follow Me. For whoever desires to save his life will lose it, but whoever loses his life for My sake will find it" (Matthew 16:24-25).

Watch!

Several times over Jesus urgently warned His disciples to maintain a posture of watchfulness. "Watch therefore, for you know neither the day nor the hour in which the Son of Man is coming" (Matthew 25:13). Jesus uttered those words after telling about the virgins who had fallen asleep while waiting for the bridegroom. "Take heed, watch and pray; for you do not know when the time is" (Mark 13:33). "And what I say to you, I say to all: Watch!" (Mark 13:37). We have a generation of equipped saints, trained for harvest, who are asleep in front of the VCR.

Turn off the TV, put away the golf clubs, and wake up. Cancel cable. Sell your TV, and give the money to the poor (Luke 12:33). Our bridegroom's return is very near. "Let your waist be girded and your lamps burning" (Luke 12:35).

Get out of Hollywood's face, and into His face.

CHAPTER SEVEN

Take Another Look At Jesus

Our faith and worship center around Jesus Christ. And yet many of us worship a Jesus we do not know very well. It is so easy to formulate wrong concepts about who Jesus is, that we begin to worship a Jesus of our own creation. The Father is calling the Church in this hour not only to a renewed *focus* upon Jesus in worship, but to an accurate *knowledge* of Jesus in worship.

As I gave myself fervently to the study of Jesus in the Gospels, I began to see Jesus in a new way. It was as though I were seeing Jesus for the first time. The Jesus I was seeing was shattering the glossy image I had erected in my mind of who I thought He was.

It is a deception to close your eyes, think of who you would like Jesus to be, and then decide you've had a revelation. There's only one way to know who Jesus really is, and that is by looking at His self-revelation to us in the holy Scriptures. We have been given a vehicle by which we now look into His face, and that is through His word.

Who Is Your Christ?

In today's religious community, it is no longer enough to be "Christ-centered." We must ask one question further: Which Christ do you serve?

A fatal disease has infected the American Church, known commonly by the term "liberalism." The liberal thinkers of this century have not only stretched the limits of Christianity, they have in fact stepped outside our faith.

It is eternally important what you believe about Jesus Christ. The Lord impressed this truth so clearly to my heart: Any time you compromise or change or deny a fundamental truth of the *personhood* of Christ, you have a new religion. His deity, His being co-eternal with the Father, His virgin birth, sinless life, atoning death for the sins of mankind, His death, burial, resurrection, ascension, and His judgment of all men, bringing to glory those He knows, and condemning to eternal judgment those who reject the only Son of God — all of these are among the fundamental doctrines of *who* Christ is. If you deny or change any of these doctrines of Christ's personhood, it is because you do not know Him. And if you do not know Christ, you do not have God, you are deceived, a blind leader of the blind, and you will receive the greater condemnation.

Second John 9 declares, "Whoever transgresses and does not abide in the doctrine of Christ does not have God." We can agree to disagree on certain nonessential doctrines, and can even embrace believers who hold differing views regarding the workings of the Holy Spirit in the world today. But we cannot agree to disagree when it comes to the doctrine of Christ. The doctrine of who Christ is is not up for discussion. Come up with another doctrine of Christ, and you have another christ. We must worship the Father in Spirit and in *truth.*

The Uniqueness Of Christ

I invite you to come with me and take another look at Jesus. I'd like you to walk with me as I recount how Jesus revealed Himself to me in an entirely new way as I immersed myself in the Gospels. I've had the practice now for several years of reading through the Gospels twice a year, but only recently did I begin to see Jesus in ways I had never seen Him before.

The more I saw Him the more I realized, "I don't think like Him, I don't act like Him, I don't talk like Him." With every page I turned, I would shake my head and say to myself, "I don't think like Him, I don't act like Him, I don't talk like Him. I am nothing like Him."

Creative Ideas

I'm always failing the Philip test. Let me explain. A multitude has been with Jesus, and He is about to feed the five thousand. "Then Jesus lifted up His eyes, and seeing a great multitude coming toward Him, He said to Philip, 'Where shall we buy bread, that these may eat?' But this He said to test him, for He Himself knew what He would do" (John 6:5-6). Jesus asked this question of Philip to test him. The answer to the test was, "Well, Lord, just take some loaves and fish and multiply them in Your hands, and we'll be able to feed everyone." How many think you would have passed that test? I know I wouldn't have come up with the right answer. I cried, "Lord, if You're testing me like that, I'm failing all the time." Instead of knowing the mighty thing that Jesus is wanting to do, I'm constantly thinking puny, doubting, limiting, earthly thoughts.

I must confess, brothers and sisters, that I have managed the church with my own understanding. I have run the business of pastoring far too confidently. We have man-made worship services, clever programs, creative outreaches, and masterful sermons. And we miss God's miraculous provision because we have no idea what wonderful thing Christ wants to do. What would happen, Lord, if just once we passed the Philip test, and really heard what You had in mind for us?

The Entrepreneur

Jesus never tried to capitalize upon His ministry successes. He never tried to use one success to build a larger success.

Take the feeding of the five thousand, for example. Now there's something worth milking. If I had been Jesus' promotional manager, by the next week I would have had twenty thousand people out. Can't you just imagine how the ads could read? "Five thousand fed with five loaves and two fish!" "Watch the Master break bread! Free meal for all observers." "Hungry? Come to the revival meeting!" You can start a magazine with this kind of stuff, Jesus. Come on, Lord, at least launch a monthly newsletter.

Watch what Jesus did. You can follow it in the record of

John's Gospel. He used the multiplication of the bread as an object lesson to bring a new revelation of Himself, saying, "I am the bread of life." He went on to say, "Unless you eat the flesh of the Son of Man and drink His blood, you have no life in you." At this, the circuits of the Jews began to overload and blow. They said, "We can't deal with this, this is a hard teaching." And so, many of His disciples stopped following Him (John 6:66). Jesus took the feeding of the five thousand, turned it around, and used it as the vehicle to cause many of His followers to fall away. I said to myself, "I am nothing like Him."

I can tell you how the Lord convicted me personally in this area. Recently I did another reprint of my book, *Exploring Worship,* and had an idea. It occurred to me to make one slight change on the cover — paste one short phrase onto the front cover, right near the top tab: "Over 50,000 sold!" Might impress somebody. Might even garner more sales. Then the Holy Spirit revealed the pride and greed of my heart, and how un-Christlike my motivations were.

In this and other ways, God has been dealing forcefully with me regarding the carnal tendency toward self-advancement. The Lord has required me to turn down some of my choicest ministry offers, in part because I knew they would put my picture in their magazine advertisements.

Working The Crowd

Jesus operated totally independently of people. Whatever He did or didn't do, it had nothing to do with those around Him. Everything He did was because it was what the Father was telling Him to do.

This is illustrated beautifully in the account of the triumphal entry into Jerusalem on the donkey. For three years Jesus has been saying to His followers, "Don't tell anyone! Keep it to yourself! Don't tell them who I am or what I've done." Now, finally, the Father gives the green light. "Go ahead, Jesus, it's time. Let them praise You."

With the children leading the way, they began to throw their branches and garments before Jesus and to cry, "Hosanna! Blessed is He who comes in the name of the Lord." If I had been Jesus, I think I would have been tempted to look around the crowd with a satisfied look that would have conveyed, "That's right, folks, go ahead. This is your moment of praise. It's time, lift your voices up. You got it right, that's exactly who I am. Let's make this a praise party for the record books."

But look at what Jesus is doing. While they're praising, He's weeping! (See Luke 19:41.) Say what? Weeping? Come on, Jesus, you're putting a damper on the meeting!

I want you to see that Jesus never got caught up in crowd euphoria. He wasn't affected by the energy of the masses. He operated totally independently of the people.

I've done virtually the opposite. In so many words, I've taught worship leaders to sense when there's a spark of excitement in a worship service, and use it to the fullest advantage. "When you a see a wave cresting in a worship service, ride that thing as fast and far as you can." The problem is, we have a generation of worship leaders who don't know what to do when the people don't respond. And we'll jump on it whenever we sense any momentum building in a congregational service, even if its origin is not of the Holy Spirit.

Worship leaders are not called to lead people in the direction they want to go. They are called to lead as they hear from the Father.

On Receiving Honor

One of Jesus' simple statements has really gripped my life: "I do not receive honor from men" (John 5:41). He did not say, "I do not solicit or seek honor from men." He didn't even say, "I am not influenced by the honor of men." He said, "When it comes, I don't even receive it."

When they said things like, "Good saying, Teacher," in His heart Jesus was thinking, "I don't receive that."

To use the greatest contrast possible, let's talk about me. I'll tell you what I do. After I've finished a sermon, I will find subtle ways to find out what others thought. I'll ask my wife, "How did the preacher do this morning?" I'll look for the nod from the church elders. I'll pay attention to how many positive comments I get afterwards. I'll take note if we sell an unusual number of sermon cassettes after the service. And after getting the pulse of how my sermon was received, I will make a determination as to its success.

Jesus, on the other hand, didn't look at the people's responses as any gauge at all of His ministry success. The only issue for Jesus was, "Did I speak what the Father told Me to say?" If the Father said, "Good job, Son, You said it just the way I wanted You to," then Jesus called that success.

I do not mean to negate the necessity of accountability and correction for the true minister of God. Every pastor and teacher needs to have those who provide constructive feedback and input into his or her ministry. If correction is necessary, I need to receive that. But I need to be careful that I not receive and feed off the praises and commendations of men.

If I do not receive honor from men, then here's the liberating part: I need not receive dishonor from men. This is what gave Jesus His incredible freedom in the presence of His critics.

I have often been amazed at how Jesus handled confrontational situations. When He went "head to head" with the Pharisees, He never backed down once. I thought, "Jesus, You sure were thick-skinned!" But it wasn't that Jesus was hard or tough; it was simply that when they fired their dishonor at Him, He didn't receive it. Because He didn't receive their honor either.

Notoriety

One of the most insidious temptations for pastors and ministers, and something that has clawed to find a hold in my soul, is the desire for notoriety. It flies under so many pious disguises: "I want to be well-known so that my message will be received." "It's good for people to see my picture, because then they can get a sense of my spirit by the expression of my countenance." "I want to advertise our event in that Christian magazine so that we can touch more people with the power of Jesus Christ." "The more that people know about me and my ministry, the more the potential to change their lives."

Look at it carefully: The desire to cultivate a large following and have one's name become a household word is completely nonexistent in Jesus' life. Say it with me, "In Jesus' name, I despise notoriety and the attention of men."

For some, ministry success is if you've written a book and are being invited to speak at ministers' conferences. You are highly esteemed by Christian leaders if you are in demand on the conference circuit. "For what is highly esteemed among men is an abomination in the sight of God" (Luke 16:15).

Jesus said, "He who speaks from himself seeks his own glory; but He who seeks the glory of the One who sent Him is true, and no unrighteousness is in Him" (John 7:18). From this statement the Lord showed me that every time I preach a message that originates from me rather than from God, in my heart I am seeking my own glory. How many times have I contoured a message so as to ensure the best possible reception, so that the pastor who invited me would say nice things about me and want me back again?

A good brother recently asked me to write a chapter for a book he was compiling with various contributing authors. After praying about it, I sensed a very light and gentle nudge to the effect of "Don't write it." The Lord didn't give me a reason, I just sensed I wasn't to write it. Then a couple weeks later I heard the book would be published by YWAM. Immediately this thought came to my mind: "YWAM? They haven't published any of my materials yet. This would be a good ministry contact." So guess what I did? I wrote the chapter. And sent it off. And guess what else I had to do, after the Holy Spirit was done with me? I had to call the brother up and say, "Pull my article." I had written it because I was seeking my own glory.

Signs And Wonders

The Lord opened my understanding to something that hinders us from moving in supernatural power and anointing. It came to me as I was meditating in John 5:44: "How can you believe, who receive honor from one another, and do not seek the honor that comes from the only God?"

The Lord spoke that verse to me in this way: "How can you believe, be a man of faith, and move in the supernatural dynamics of faith, when you receive the honor of men? How can I trust you with a supernatural endowment, because you know that people will always make a fuss over someone who is used of God in demonstrations of the miraculous. I can't allow people to fuss over you like that when your flesh is receiving their attention."

I realized that moving in kingdom power requires that we come to terms with this issue. God will give faith only to those who are unwilling to receive honor from men, but who diligently seek the honor of God.

Jesus And Money

In the way Jesus handled and talked about money, He communicated only disdain. In fact, not once does the Bible record that Jesus ever handled a coin. He delegated the purse to Judas Iscariot (even though He knew Judas was a thief). When He wanted to illustrate a point, He had to say, "Show me a coin," because He didn't have one on His person. When Peter needed tax money, He sent Peter to get a coin from the mouth of a fish. It's almost as though He took measures to avoid even touching the stuff.

Jesus described money with two rather uncompliment-ary phrases: "unrighteous mammon" (Luke 16:9), and "the deceitfulness of riches" (Matthew 13:22).

If you're rich, and you're thinking about coming to Christ, think twice. Jesus is still saying to people today, "Sell all that you have and distribute to the poor, and you will have treasure in heaven; and come, follow Me" (Luke 18:22). If you're rich and you want to follow Jesus, you're going to have to do like Zacchaeus, and divest yourself of your wealth.

You can't get into heaven and keep all that money. Jesus called it "impossible" (Luke 18:24-27). Your money owns your affections. You can't have your heart on the Kingdom and hold onto your money at the same time (Matthew 6:24).

Wealth's Deceitfulness

Money is deceitful. It wraps its slimy little tentacles around your heart, and wins your fond affection. The Holy Spirit helps you to become aware of it, and so you do something violent to loosen its hold on your heart. Then you relax, because you think you've gained the victory over money and materialism — which means you're now deceived. The deceit of wealth has you convinced that you've conquered the allurement of money, and now you're blind to your materialism.

I don't care how many years you've known Christ, you must continually evaluate your relationship to money. If you have the fear of God in you, there is nothing healthier than coming to a place of basic distrust in your heart attitudes toward money.

The Holy Spirit pricked my heart about this recently. Our church offerings had fallen off a little at one point, and so I decided we needed to include more scriptural exhortations and teachings on giving when it was offering time. After all, doesn't every loving pastor want to instruct His flock in the joys and benefits of scriptural giving? But the Holy Spirit revealed my heart: I wasn't preaching in order to nurture and instruct the flock, I was preaching to increase the offerings.

Freedom From Materialism

How can we purify our heart attitudes toward money? Thankfully, Jesus gave us a very clear solution, and guess what — it's not tithing. If you're not tithing, you are completely bound in greed and materialism. But what about the tithing Christian who battles with materialism, what is he to do? The answer is in Luke 11:41, "But rather give alms of such things as you have, then indeed all things are clean to you."

Alms are gifts to poor people. Simply stated, Jesus was saying "almsgiving purifies." The Pharisees were arguing with Jesus, and the subject of the controversy was, "What is it that cleanses a person?" The Pharisees said, "Washing hands before meals purifies." Jesus said, "Nope. Almsgiving purifies."

What does almsgiving cleanse us from? Materialism and greed. Every time you sense money wanting to find a little place in your heart, give a chunk away to a needy saint who will never be able to repay you.

When surveyed, do you know what Christians here in the U.S. say is their number one temptation? Coming before pride, self-centeredness, anger, sexual lust, envy, lying, gluttony, etc., the foremost confessed temptation for Christians is *materialism.*

Listen carefully, dear materialistic saints. Every believer should be functioning in the blessed virtue of almsgiving. We have allowed the Welfare System here in America to rob us of a blessing. We think, "They're being taken care of," and so we neglect that which would purify us of the encroachments of materialism. One reason the American Church is so weighed down with worldliness and materialism is because we have not been properly taught about almsgiving.

The Priority Of Eternity

There is only one thing that Jesus valued. If it was eternal, He placed great importance on it. If it was for this life only (like money), He brushed it off with indifferent contempt.

After studying the Gospels nonstop for three weeks, I suddenly saw what the essence of the gospel was. I claim to be a preacher of the gospel, but my preaching covers so many topics that at times the message of the gospel can seem to become complicated.

What is the gospel? If you had but two minutes with someone, and you wanted to share the heartbeat of the gospel, what would you say?

The gospel, in a nutshell, is "eternal life." Jesus came to bring us life, abundant life, eternal life. It took me three weeks to come back to John 3:16!

Jesus came from outside time to try to get it through to us that there is infinitely more to life than these eighty-or-so years we might expect to spend on this planet. All of us are careening toward an eternity. The world is seeking self-actualization in this life, but Jesus came with the message that the way of life is actually the way of death. "For whoever desires to save his life will lose it, but whoever loses his life for My sake will save it" (Luke 9:24).

Lukewarm Love

I have been greatly impacted with how often Jesus issued warnings to His listeners. One attitude of mine that the words of Jesus have really straightened out has been my general attitude of, "Well, if you're not ready to deal with that problem area in your life right now, that's no big problem. The Holy Spirit will get you. Give Him time."

There are some individuals toward whom I have actually had this kind of attitude: "The Lord loves him, and even though he's living in a backslidden condition, I know the Lord is going to get ahold of him. He'll come around in time." So I would just release him to the Lord, and pray for him. But the urgency in Jesus' words have shown me we don't have time.

Jesus said, "Watch therefore, for you know neither the day nor the hour in which the Son of Man is coming" (Matthew 25:13). Everything Jesus says calls out, "Today! Now! Watch! Beware!"

I have exhorted, I have encouraged, I have taught, but I realize that I have done little warning. Folks, we don't have time. Jesus is coming back any moment. *Today* is the day of salvation. We must speak urgently to those whose love has grown lukewarm. They are teetering on the precipice of hell, and we as shepherds, brothers, and sisters carry the sober responsibility of warning them.

Part Three:

Expressions of Intimacy

CHAPTER EIGHT

Holy Emotions

In the time of the American colonies, God revealed Himself in a mighty way one day to a certain seventeen-year-old lad. God gave him a profound revelation from a single Scripture, 1 Timothy 1:17: "Now to the King eternal, immortal, invisible, to God who alone is wise, be honor and glory forever and ever. Amen." This young man wrote in his journal, "There came into my soul a sense of the glory of the Divine Being different from anything I had ever experienced before. I prayed to God that I might enjoy Him, and prayed with a new sort of affection."

God sparked off an intimate relationship with that young man, using him singularly in a revival that swept through the American colonies — we refer to that revival as "The Great Awakening." Perhaps you have already guessed that I am speaking of Jonathan Edwards.

Holy Affections

Although Jonathan Edwards is perhaps best known for his famous sermon, "Sinners in the Hands of an Angry God," his ministry was not centered upon judgment and the wrath of God. The central theme of his preaching was that of having an affectionate relationship with God. Jonathan Edwards has been credited by some as the greatest mind America has yet produced, and yet the focus of this brilliant man's message was to call believers beyond an intellectual embracing of God to a heartfelt delight in beholding the beauty of the Lord.

Edwards taught that the essence of a true spiritual experience is to be overwhelmed by a glimpse of the beauty of God, to be drawn to the glory of His perfection, and to sense His irresistible love. He wrote, "The holy Scriptures do everywhere place religion very much in the affections; such as fear, hope, love, hatred, desire, joy, sorrow, gratitude, compassion, and zeal." He also said, "He who has no religious affection is in a state of spiritual death and is wholly destitute of powerful quickening influences of the Spirit of God."

Emotional Versus Soulish

Many people are talking today about having "passion" in one's relationship with Jesus. Jonathan Edwards used the word "affections." For the purposes of this chapter, I'd like to use the word "emotions." God desires to have an *emotional* relationship with His people.

I understand you might have a problem with that word. Passion, yes; affections, yes; but emotions? I've heard many disparaging remarks about our emotions. "Let's not get carried away with our emotions." "We don't want any emotional responses around here, we want the real thing." Have you forgotten the Scripture that says, "Bless the Lord, O my *soul*; And all that is within me, bless His holy name!" (Psalm 103:1)?

"Your style of praise is simply emotionalism," they complain. True praise is not emotionalism, but it is emotional. Your emotions are not evil. They were given to you by God for holy purposes.

I would like to distinguish between what is "emotional" and what is "soulish." Emotions without the Spirit is soul. Emotions with the Spirit is passion.

Anything that is truly of God always begins in your spirit. But if your spirit is deeply touched, it will inevitably affect your soul, setting off cascading waves of glorious emotions. And if your soul is deeply touched, it will inevitably affect your body. You'll want to do something with your body — kneel, dance, weep, lift hands, etc. When God's Spirit breaks on you, that wave of His presence will wash over your entire being — spirit, soul, and body.

Some people think that if we respond emotionally to a

sermon or a call of the Spirit that our responses will be shallow and short-lived. To the contrary, if our response to the Spirit is not deeply emotional, then it will be ephemeral and will fizzle quickly. Too many of our spiritual commitments don't last because they never touched us deeply enough to get into our emotions. If your spirit is moved by God to such an extent that it spills over into your soul, you are more likely to make a long-lasting change.

The Controversy

Jonathan Edwards himself tried to warn the colonists against sheer emotionalism. But when the power of God hit the colonies over 200 years ago, it set off all kinds of emotional displays. Critics called it "froth" and "disorder." The churches were divided over the revival. It squarely split the Presbyterian church in America. Some were for, some against. And can you guess what the issue was? People were getting emotional in church! They were actually displaying spiritual fervor in the house of God!

This has been, in fact, the bone of contention in virtually every revival that has visited the Church. We don't mind people getting saved and baptized in water, but we can't handle it when they get passionate as they behold the face of God.

It is well documented that most revivals have been accompanied by a fresh vitality in congregational singing. Luther's reforms were accompanied by a resurgence in singing, many of the songs being written by Luther himself. The preacher John Wesley was aided by his brother, songwriter Charles Wesley. Billy Sunday traveled with Homer Rodeheaver. (Now there's a name for the pregnant moms to consider.) D.L. Moody's revival meetings included dynamic singing led by Ira D. Sankey. And the list goes on.

Revival Fire

Why has a revitalization of singing always attended true revival? The answer lies in the fact that singing is the mouthpiece of the soul. When God moves in revival fire, and fires up your emotions, you want to sing! Let me go one step further:

You can't have a current of Holy Ghost revival without a wave of holy emotions cresting in the hearts of God's people.

Listen to what a friend wrote of the meetings held by William & Catherine Booth, the founders of the Salvation Army: "Some people were offended at the tremendous 'Amens' and shouts of victory which prevailed on every side...The noise was sometimes tremendous — but God was in it."

There was a lot of energy in D.L. Moody's meetings as well. During Moody's two-year crusade in Great Britain, Queen Victoria attended one of the meetings. Although a devout believer, the Queen had this to say about the revival service: "I am sure that they are very good and sincere people, but it is not the sort of religious performance which I like." Unfortunately, believers are still looking at the red-hot zeal that accompanies the genuine move of the Spirit of God, and dismissing it with words like, "That's okay for them, but it's just not my style."

John Wesley once said, "Give me one hundred preachers who fear nothing but sin and desire nothing but God and I care not a straw whether they be clergy or laymen; such alone will shake the gates of hell and set up the Kingdom of heaven on earth."

A Sound Mind

Second Timothy 1:7 makes this powerful declaration: "For God has not given us a spirit of fear, but of power and of love and of a sound mind." The original Greek word for "sound mind" signifies "entire command of the passions and desires." It conveys the idea of having a constant handle on one's emotions.

Some people's emotions are sometimes like a runaway train. It's almost as though they stand outside of themselves and watch while their emotions escalate. But the Spirit of God has been given to us so that we might gain control over every aspect of our soul (see Galatians 5:23).

I have three things to say about our emotions.

1. Our emotions are God-given

God Himself is deeply emotional, and He has made us in His image. Why did He intend for us to be emotional? So that we might be able to return the emotions He lavishes upon us, enjoying a reciprocating, passionate, face-to-face relationship with Him.

The emotion of fear is a gift of God. We teach our children to fear the stove, because if it's hot they can hurt themselves badly. The emotion of concern or care is a gift from God. What if we didn't care about going to work, paying the bills, putting food on the table, or attending to the work of God? Anger is a gift — thank God you can get mad. (How many have a lot to be thankful for?) God intended that we should get mad at the devil, mad at sin, and mad at temptation. And He has given us a way to express that anger in prayer.

2. We must control how we express our emotions

Sin distorted our emotions. After sin entered mankind, listen to Adam's first words: "I was afraid because I was naked; and I hid myself." That emotion of fear which had been a gift from God, useful for so many noble purposes, was now twisted by sin and so distorted that it became the very thing which pulled Adam away from the presence of God.

Our emotions, originally a gift from God, now have two possibilities. They can be an asset or a liability, depending on how we direct them. Every emotion we possess now carries the potential to help or hinder us in our walk with God, and thus must be carefully controlled.

One graphic example of this is in the area of our sexual passions and desires. Our sexual desires, when expressed properly within the confines of the marriage covenant, are a source of great delight and blessing and fruitfulness. But allowed to be expressed outside of marriage, and those same passions become a source of incredible destruction and grief.

3. Controlled emotions are a great asset

Emotions are mobilizers, they move us to action. A mother of a young child hears car tires screeching out in the street, and you should watch that mother move! The instantaneous emotions that fill her heart have her breaking all speed records to find out why a car is stopping suddenly outside.

In the same way, emotions move us to work for God. Think for a moment of an area of ministry in which you serve. You probably serve because you have some emotional feelings about the needs of that ministry. Talk to someone who is involved in the pro-life movement, and you'll detect some emotion in their face. Watch an evangelist as he conducts an altar call, and you'll see the emotions that motivate his life.

Emotions In Worship

Similarly, our emotions move us to worship, which explains clearly why there is so much resistance to displays of emotion in church. It's because the devil is out to strip the expression of holy emotions from the house of God. If he can plunder the people of God of their emotional freedom, he will defuse our worship, robbing us of our joy, sapping us of strength (Nehemiah 8:10), and thus stealing our victory. We're doing the devil's work when we attempt to stifle God's Spirit-filled saints from expressing their emotions openly and exuberantly.

Somebody says, "Well, I'm just not an emotional person." Wrong. Every one of us is created by God to be intensely emotional. But some of us have learned to repress our emotions.

I think we men are particularly guilty here. It's amazing to me how many greeting cards from husbands to their wives start off with an apology. "I know I don't say it as often as I should..." It's hard to buy a card for your wife that isn't an apology. And here's the amazing part: Men buy those cards! Why? Because many of us have come to think it's masculine to be unemotional, inexpressive, and stoically aloof.

You Can Do It

If you have difficulty expressing your emotions, allow me to preach the gospel here for a moment: Jesus came to change you! He came to change your heart, your attitudes, and your personality. I read a newspaper clipping a couple years ago about a study by the National Institute on Aging.

Their research showed that a person's personality is pretty much molded by age 30. Growth and maturity after 30 take place within the framework of a personality that "is set like plaster." Change thereafter takes "extraordinary, heroic" efforts, they said. What their research didn't take into account was the transforming power of Christ resident within the believer. Thank God that He still changes us.

Beloved, when you get a glimpse of what Jesus has done for you, you'll get emotional. When you understand what Jesus did for you at Calvary, what His blood provides for you today, and the status you enjoy as a king and a priest in His immediate presence, you'll have some holy affections arise in your soul. My, if you don't get excited about Jesus, what will it take?

It's a lie of the devil belched out of the pit of hell that says emotions don't belong in the house of God. If the devil can freeze your emotions, he knows he'll freeze you — you'll be useless for God.

Directed Emotions

When your face is set toward the Lord, when your spirit is poised to worship the Lord, let your emotions go. When you're in the presence of God, that's the time to release your heart in loving abandon. And when your soul is pointed in the wrong direction, for instance in anger against your spouse or child or another person, that's the time to pull your emotions in with the enabling of the Holy Spirit.

Our problem is, we have the thing inverted. When our soul is facing something potentially sinful, we're very quick to release our emotions. And when our soul is poised in praise or intercession, we stand before God like hardened stones. Listen, my friend. When you're in the place of prayer, allow the infinite emotions of the Holy Spirit to grip your soul, firing up your intercession in a godly fervor.

Some people complain about their worship leaders: "I don't understand why that worship team has to try to make something happen every Sunday. They're always stirring it up, stirring it up." Hey, that's their job. The goal of a church's worship ministry is to stir up the holy affections of God's people.

CHAPTER NINE

Beholding His Beauty

One thing I have desired of the Lord, that will I seek:
That I may dwell in the house of the Lord all the days of
my life, to behold the beauty of the Lord, and to inquire
in His temple. (Psalm 27:4)

To behold the beauty (literally, "delightfulness") of the Lord is to gaze upon His character and personhood. I want to direct your meditation today to just three aspects of the Lord's beauty.

1. He is beautiful in power

The Scriptures call Him "omnipotent," "Almighty," the all-powerful One. In other words, there ain't nothin' He can't do. He spoke the worlds into existence with the word of His mouth. His exceeding power has been most forcibly demonstrated in the resurrection of His Son from the grave.

God is so powerful, even His presence is overpowering. You may recall the time when the angel rolled the stone away from before Christ's tomb, and the Roman guards fainted on the spot. They fell out like dead men at the presence of one angel. But the presence of an angel doesn't even compare with the power that emanates from God's presence.

Actually, this is the very thing that posed a problem for God. God said, "I want to have a personal, intimate relationship with man, but anytime I get close to them, they fry." Our relationship with God was at a veritable impasse. That's why

God came up with the plan of redemption, and sent His Son to this planet. Now a way has been made, through the flesh of God's Son, for us to have access to the immediate presence of God. Ah, thank God for Jesus!

When Jesus comes back, you don't want to be an unbeliever. Because the Bible says that when Jesus returns, He will destroy His enemies with the sheer splendor of His presence (2 Thessalonians 2:8). Jesus says, "I'll tell you how I'm going to take care of my enemies. I'm just going to show up."

Take a moment to behold the beauty of His power.

2. He is beautiful in sovereignty

The sovereignty of God means this: God does what He wants, when He wants, without asking anyone's permission.

Mind you, I have volunteered my consulting services to God on more than one occasion. "Lord, if You'd like a little input on how to run things, let me know." I let Him know I was particularly willing to give Him feedback on how to run my life. Interesting thing is, though, He never took me up on the offer.

It's funny, but God seems to think He can do whatever He wants. Psalm 115:3 says God's in heaven, so He does whatever He pleases. He must think He's God or something!

Have you ever felt like you were the victim of His sovereignty? I'm sure Job did. I think Paul did too.

One day God came to Paul. "I've got a gift for you, Paul."

"A gift? For me? Wow! What is it?"

"Here," God said, handing Paul a nicely wrapped present. "Open it."

Paul carefully undid the ribbon, pulled back the wrapping, lifted the lid, and — a demon! God gave Paul a demon! That's what 2 Corinthians 12:7 says: "...a thorn in the flesh was given to me, a messenger of Satan to buffet me." Three times Paul pled with the Lord for it to be taken away, but the Lord's response to him was, "My grace is sufficient for you, for My strength is made perfect in weakness" (2 Corinthians 12:9).

It's true that God sometimes does things in our lives that we don't understand, but still His sovereignty is beautiful, awesome, to be admired, examined, and contemplated.

Won't you take a moment to reflect on His sovereignty?

3. He is beautiful in holiness

There are certain creatures that God has placed in the fire of His immediate presence. The Bible calls them "seraphim". All they ever do, night and day, is cry, "Holy holy holy is the Lord of hosts; The whole earth is full of His glory!" (Isaiah 6:3).

These seraphim are absolutely sinless, flawless creatures. And yet of these very creatures the Bible says, "In the council of the holy ones God is greatly feared" (Psalm 89:7, NIV). It also says, "he is more awesome than all who surround him."

These seraphim are a study. They're covered with eyes all over—above their wings, beside their wings, under their wings, eyes everywhere. I believe this speaks of extreme intelligence. They are probably the wisest of all God's creatures. And yet what do we find these creatures of incredible brainpower applying themselves to? They're not debating the finer points of existential philosophy — "I think, therefore I am." They're doing but one thing: worshiping the holiness of Him who sits on the throne.

Worship is one of the smartest things you'll ever do. If you have half a brain, you too will fall before Him who is seated on the throne, and cry, "Holy holy holy!"

The holiness of God is a complex concept, and carries three ideas with it:

- Completeness. Wholeness. When God makes us holy, He makes us whole. To be holy is to be everything God intended us to be.
- Purity. Holiness is the purifying process in our lives in which we become more and more like Jesus. As the fire burns away the dross of our sinfulness, we desire the gold of our hearts to become so pure that when God looks upon us He is able to see His own reflection in us.
- Uncommonness. In the pantheon of heaven's hosts, God stands out from all other beings as singularly eminent and uniquely peerless. In this sense the opposite of holiness is not so much sin as it is commonness. The more like God we are, the greater we stand out in contrast to the world.

What a privilege, to gaze upon the holiness of our God! He is entirely complete, absolutely pure, and singularly uncommon.

How To Say It?

O the beauty of the Lord! The biblical writers fumbled for words, stuttering as it were to describe with the human tongue the awesome majesty of our God. Under inspiration of the Holy Spirit they called Him "Most Mighty," "Most Holy," "Most High God," "Everlasting Father," "Lord God Almighty," "Lord of Hosts," "the Holy One of Israel," "Mighty God of heaven," "Ancient of Days," "our Lord and Savior Jesus Christ," "Captain of the Lord's Hosts," "Image of the Invisible God," "King of Glory," "Lion of the Tribe of Judah," "King of kings and Lord of lords," "Blessed and Only Potentate."

Little wonder that Moses cried, "Who is like You, O Lord, among the gods? Who is like You, glorious in holiness, fearful in praises, doing wonders?" (Exodus 15:11).

"Let the beauty of the Lord our God be upon us" (Psalm 90:17).

Face To Face

Here's the incredible part. This great God, who is beautiful in power, beautiful in sovereignty, and beautiful in holiness, invites you and me to a "face-to-face" relationship with Him.

Those mighty seraphim who serve in God's immediate presence were given six wings — two for flying, two for covering their feet, and two for covering their face (Isaiah 6:2). But not so with you. You are invited to come with an open face to gaze upon the beauty of the Lord.

Revelation 20:11 predicts that heaven and earth will flee away from His face. And it is before this magnificent face that we come.

In His mercy, God has given us "shades" so that we can behold His glory without perishing. "For now we see through a glass, darkly; but then face to face" (1 Corinthians 13:12, KJV). God has placed a protective shield before us so that we can look upon His face. If seeing Him now is this glorious, can you imagine what it will be like to behold Him when the dark glass is taken away?

Eye Level

Sometimes I will motion my wife, Marci, to come over to a step, and by now she knows what I have in mind. She is shorter than me by enough that when she stands a step above me, we're eye to eye. It's just the right height for a great embrace. Similarly, God has elevated us up to eye level. Sometimes we bow our heads in His presence, and that certainly is fitting; sometimes we raise our face to Him, and that is great. But I want you to see that you can gaze upon His beauty straight ahead, face to face. He has raised you to His level.

Not only does God *offer* this face-to-face relationship — He *wants* it! Jesus said that the Father is *actively seeking* those who will worship Him in Spirit and in truth (John 4:23).

Hear the Father seeking true worshipers as He calls to us, "O my dove, in the clefts of the rock, in the secret places of the cliff, let me see your face, let me hear your voice; for your voice is sweet, and your face is lovely" (Song of Solomon 2:14). Will you respond to His imploring cry? Will you bring your face before His? Will your voice be heard?

Spirit Empowering

Perhaps there is a cry in your heart for a fresh passion for the face of Jesus. I don't mean this to be a theological statement at all — but just get baptized all over again in the Holy Spirit! Seek to be filled anew with the Spirit, for He has been given to us to rekindle our passion for Jesus. When you get baptized with the Holy Spirit and fire, beloved, you'll know some godly passion. The baptism of the Holy Spirit is an experience that will catapult you into a new freedom of expressing holy emotions in the presence of the Lord.

The Holy Spirit is infinitely emotional. The fruit of the Spirit are chock-full of emotion. Love, joy, peace... they all glisten with passion. I like to refer to them as "passion fruit."

God wants you to be passionate in your relationship with Him. He said, "When you come into My presence, come with

thanksgiving. Come with praise" (see Psalm 100). Thanksgiving is an emotional expression. Praise is passionate. God is
saying, "When you come into My presence, come with passion
and emotion. Get in My face — passionately!"

The eyes are the most expressive part of the body. If you
really want to know what someone is thinking, read the expression in his or her eyes. That's why many believers avoid
eye contact with God. They're ashamed for God to look into
their eyes and see how lackluster their love for Him really
is.

What Charges Your Battery?

Awhile back, I read of a man who individually interviewed
350 Christian leaders around the United States as part of a
research project. At the end of his travels he made a statement that grabbed my heart with conviction: "I found a great
deal of zeal for God's work, but very little passion for God."
Ouch.

Have you discovered that trying to spend time with Jesus
from a guilt motivation never works? Our relationship with
Jesus will never be satisfying as long as we cram in time with
Him because we feel we ought to. It is when we come to the
positive motivation of wanting Him, desiring His presence,
yearning to know Him more intimately and personally, that
our walk with Him will ignite. Oh Lord, give us a passion to
know You.

Something that was so obvious in the life of Jesus while
He was on earth was His preoccupation to be alone with the
Father. He mixed with the masses because that's what He
was called to do, but what He really wanted to do was to be
with His Father. The closest thing to anxiety I see in Jesus
(other than in Gethsemane) is when He has been with the
multitudes for the day, and He pulls Himself away from them
with an urgency that suggests, "I've got to get away and be
with My Father."

Jesus lived for those moments with the Father. As for me,
I have the whole thing inverted. I spend time with the Father
because I know it's necessary if I'm going to do what really
pumps me — that is, ministering to the people. I'm more energized by serving Him than being with Him. Too many of us

are more satisfied with working for God than with knowing God.

Jesus wasn't even energized by demonstrations of the supernatural. For example, on one occasion Jesus climbed into a boat with His disciples, knowing that a storm would come up and that He would calm the storm with a word. If I were Jesus, do you know what I'd be doing? I'd be sitting there thinking to myself, "Only a few hours to go, guys, and you're going to see a good one. I can hardly wait to see the looks on your faces when I still the wind and waves!" But what is Jesus doing? Sleeping. Power demonstrations didn't charge His battery. The only thing that excited Jesus was fellowshiping with His Father.

What primes your pump? What motivates you? Pastor, is it when you preach a bell-ringer of a sermon? Worship leader, is it when the worship service you're leading really sizzles? Do you delight to be a full-time salaried minister because now you have the luxury of spending even more time than ever in the secret place with Jesus?

For those who are willing, God will set your motivations and aspirations in right priority. It will be a painful work, for He will have to bring you to a place of such desperate dependence upon Him that the only cry of your heart will be, "I must gain Christ!" Only then will you realize that being in His face is your solitary source of survival.

CHAPTER TEN

The Enemy's Design

The enemy's design is to keep you out of God's face. The provision of the cross is to bring you into His presence.

Sin produces two emotional by-products in our souls. Satan is a master at massaging these devastating emotions into our souls, not only to inflict suffering, but to inhibit our growth in the grace of Christ and to erode our ability to make war in the cause of Christ.

Guilt

The first consequence of sin is guilt. No one reading these words needs guilt to be defined or explained — it has burned in all of us, at times accusing, now belittling, now jeering. Because of guilt we feel worthless and unacceptable to God.

Guilt attacks where there has been genuine sin. And that's where guilt finds its power, because our sin is very real, and our guilt is most deserved. Deserved, that is, until the application of the blood of Jesus.

The blood of Jesus, when applied to our hearts, frees us from all guilt. Romans 5:9 says we have been "justified by His blood." To be justified is to be made just, holy, without fault. When the blood of Jesus has touched someone's life, for that person "there is therefore now no condemnation" (Romans 8:1). When God justifies us, He doesn't simply pretend that our sin is gone; He removes our sin so completely from us that in His eyes we are as one who has never sinned! Thanks be to God, guilt has no legal habitation in the soul of the believer.

God has removed your guilt so that you might come into His presence and minister to Him. The blood of Jesus has revolutionized how God views you. Revelation 1:6 says God "has made us kings and priests." As a priest it is my privilege to serve in His temple, to minister to Him, to bless His name. But God doesn't want trash ministering to Him, He wants royalty attending Him. So He says, "Tell you what, I'll make you a king as well." Now don't get haughty, Christian. It's true that you're a king, but He's still the "King of kings."

Accused Before God

Then I heard a loud voice saying in heaven, "Now salvation, and strength, and the kingdom of our God, and the power of His Christ have come, for the accuser of our brethren, who accused them before our God day and night, has been cast down. And they overcame him by the blood of the Lamb and by the word of their testimony, and they did not love their lives to the death." (Revelation 12:10-11)

We know who the accuser is. It's interesting where he accuses God's people — "before our God." Have you noticed that Satan doesn't bother to accuse you until you try to come into God's presence? Stay at home on Sunday morning and you'll have a lovely, guilt-free morning. Go to church, and just listen to the accusations! "I feel like such a hypocrite. I can't believe I'm sitting here in church. I'm a Pharisee, pretending all this spiritual stuff." (The enemy always accuses us in the first person, as though they were our own thoughts, when in reality they are his thoughts injected into our minds.)

Let me tell you why the enemy steps up his accusations when you try to worship the Lord. It's because he knows that worship is transformational. Satan knows that if you get into God's presence and are truly renewed in the Spirit, that things will start to change in your life. You can't tap into the power of God and remain unchanged. But if the accuser can keep you from worshiping, he's got you bound and trapped in your sin.

Guilt is a vicious cycle. When we feel guilty from our sin, we pull back from God's presence. When we pull back from

God's presence, we struggle with sinning even more. And with more sin comes more guilt. So the cycle only deepens. Guilt is an unending whirlpool that is designed by the enemy to suck you down into spiritual destruction.

Satan will do anything to destroy your confidence to come before God. Like a wolf, his tactic is to "isolate and separate." (Perhaps you've seen this tactic of predators on a wildlife program.) Satan's scheme is to batter and barrage your soul until you pull away from the worship life of the congregation. He makes you think, "It would be hypocritical for me to go to church and worship today." If he can convince you to isolate yourself from the flow of spiritual life that happens in the gathering of the saints, you're lunch.

The purpose of guilt is to keep you from God's presence. But Jesus says, "Hang out with me. Stay in my presence, and things will start to change."

Three Kinds Of Warfare

There are three kinds of spiritual warfare. We hear most frequently, perhaps, about *offensive warfare.* Jesus described His church as being on the offensive when He said that the gates of hell would not prevail (Matthew 16:18). Gates don't attack, gates defend. Jesus pictured the church as attacking hell's gates. When it comes to spiritual warfare, I'm a firm believer in the words of Jesus, "It is more blessed to give than receive."

The second kind of warfare doesn't get the same publicity, but is perhaps a more realistic element in the everyday life of the believer, and that is *defensive warfare.* Make no mistake, hell is out to destroy every one of us. This is not a prom, folks, this is a war. Every believer must adopt a defensive stance against the strategy of the enemy, determining not to surrender a single inch of spiritual progress. The New Testament summarizes this defensive posture with two words: "stand" (Ephesians 6:13) and "resist" (James 4:7). God has never purposed for us to be passive in the face of the enemy's attack. God allows us to suffer assault in order that we might learn to rise up, take hold of the shield of faith, and apply the victory of Calvary to our lives. Without a battle there can be no victory.

The third kind of spiritual warfare gets talked about very little, but I will choose to describe it with the term *internal warfare*. This is when God contends with His enemies that are still residing within us. If you've ever been on the platform during a worship service, you've seen the war. You can watch the pained expressions as people fight with God.

Little wonder some people don't come to church. They have no intention of changing, and they'd rather not take the heat.

Some believers don't understand the power of God's presence. Virtue flows to our entire being simply by being in His presence. I have used just about every device known to pastors to try to get some people out to church. Because in my heart I know that if they'll come, things will change. I want to plead with them, "Just come!"

Some sins are overcome by applying specific principles of Christian living, but some sins are conquered primarily by spending large quantities of time before God's face. Many saints have testified to me that as they were faithful to get into God's presence, they didn't know exactly when or how it happened, but they suddenly realized that they weren't struggling with that area of sin anymore.

I like to think of getting into God's presence as "radiation treatments." The "cancer" of sin in our lives is dissipated as we spend time in the "radiation" of His presence. What most of us need is a "time exposure" to God's glory.

Conviction Or Condemnation?

Conviction is the voice of the Holy Spirit as He beckons us to turn from our sinfulness. Condemnation is the voice of the enemy as he inflames our feelings of guilt, seeking to incarcerate us in sinful patterns. The problem is, both voices come to us in the same sphere — the spirit realm. And they can sound very similar to the untrained ear. How can we discern between the voice of conviction and the voice of condemnation?

A tree is known by its fruit. You can tell the difference between conviction and condemnation by looking at the direction it's taking you. Conviction (the voice of the Spirit) points us toward repentance, which releases the grace of God in us, and motivates us to grow in the knowledge of Christ. Condemnation (the voice of the enemy) drives us to despair, which in turn feeds the sin cycle, and further debilitates our ability to function as a Christian. So ask yourself, "Am I motivated or debilitated?" Conviction always draws you into God's presence. Condemnation always pushes you away from God. By looking at the direction you're going, you can know whether it's conviction or condemnation.

Shame

The blood of Jesus has dealt the decisive blow against guilt, for now we have complete access to the presence of God. But there is a second consequence of sin that hinders many of us, and that is shame. Let me distinguish between guilt and shame with a couple illustrations.

It was *guilt* that caused Adam and Eve to hide from God, but it was *shame* that caused them to cover themselves with fig leaves. Shame is the embarrassment we feel over our failures.

To distinguish between the two again, suppose yourself to be President of the United States of America. You have been impeached for reprehensible conduct, and just before your trial you are granted a presidential pardon by your replacement, the new President. To be pardoned means to be without guilt. Now guilt-free, you can walk anywhere in America as a free man. No one will ever try to arrest you; your guilt has been completely removed.

But whereas a presidential pardon can remove guilt, it can never remove shame. As long as you live you will carry the shame of your conduct.

Now here's the wonder of the blood of Jesus: His blood cleanses us not only from guilt, but also from shame! No longer do we have to "cover up" in His presence. He invites us to come before Him with an open, unveiled face (see 2 Corinthians 3:18).

It's one thing to know you're forgiven; it's another thing altogether to feel forgiven. No amount of talking will convince you otherwise when you feel ashamed. But the blood of Jesus has provided even for those feelings of shame.

The Shedding And Sprinkling Of Blood

The tenth chapter of Hebrews distinguishes between two distinct applications of the blood of Jesus. In verse 19, the blood of Jesus gives us boldness to enter the Holiest: "Therefore, brethren, having boldness to enter the Holiest by the blood of Jesus..." That refers to the application of the blood to our lives when we are made new creatures in Christ. When the blood of Jesus is over our lives, we always have boldness to come before Him no matter how much we might struggle from day to day. This application of Christ's blood is once for all.

The second application of the blood is described three verses later: "Let us draw near with a true heart in full assurance of faith, having our hearts sprinkled from an evil conscience and our bodies washed with pure water" (Hebrews 10:22). This "sprinkling" is an application of the blood that is available to the believer on a repeated, ongoing basis. In fact, Peter says that we were called of God and sanctified by the Spirit for two purposes: so that we might walk in obedience and be sprinkled by the blood of Jesus (see 1 Peter 1:2).

Correspondingly, in the Old Testament there was the *shedding* of blood and the *sprinkling* of blood. The shedding of Christ's blood deals with our guilt before God, and the sprinkling of His blood deals with our feelings of shame and uncleanness. The book of Hebrews says this sprinkling cleanses us "from an evil conscience." In other words, you *feel* forgiven. You don't just know it mentally, you actually feel clean.

There is a sprinkling of blood for you today, dear one. Join me in this simple prayer:

> *Dear heavenly Father, I thank You that the blood of Jesus has qualified me to come into Your presence today. But I am asking to be sprinkled afresh by Your blood just now. Cleanse me from every defiling thing. Purify me from the contamination of the world. Cleanse my conscience, dissolve all guilt and shame. I receive Your cleansing right now, and rejoice in the magnificent provision of Your cross. Blessed be Your most holy name!*

Ah, for this we were created! Don't let the devil rip you off. Christ has made every provision, through His blood, for you to revel in His embrace and enjoy the ultimate right of sonship — beholding His face.

CHAPTER ELEVEN

Praise Prayers

One of the most challenging verses in the Bible is Psalm 34:1, "I will bless the Lord at *all times*; His praise shall *continually* be in my mouth." My question is simply this: How do you do that? How do you praise the Lord without ever stopping?

As though to add insult to injury, the apostle Paul writes this injunction, "pray without ceasing" (1 Thessalonians 5:17). Now I'm really in trouble. I've got to praise continually, and I've got to pray without ever stopping. Yikes.

Some of us have to go to work, God.

Has it ever happened to you while at work that you got so absorbed in your responsibilities that you stopped praising the Lord? Have you ever gotten so distracted with driving through traffic that you actually stopped praying for a couple minutes? Have you ever slept?

"Well, then, woe to you, you slovenly excuse for a Christian!" comes the voice of the accuser. Guilt and condemnation overflow as we feel like abject failures. We can't even pray without ceasing!

Why has the Holy Spirit placed such a seemingly insurmountable challenge before us? So we can all live in frustration and defeat?

A Diagram Of Prayer

The key to these questions is to be found in a proper understanding of the biblical word "prayer."

I want you to complete a diagram, so set this book down for a minute if you need to, and go find a pen or pencil. The facing page is blank, and that's where you're going to complete your diagram.

I'd like you to write down on the blank page all the ways you can think of that we express ourselves to God. Think of the ways we express ourselves to God in our corporate gatherings, as well as in the secret place alone with God. Whether it's a spoken expression, or a sung one, or a silent one, write it down. (Now for those who need a hint, your list could include words such as singing, praise, thanksgiving, worship, adoration, petition, weeping, laughing, meditation, supplication, intercession, travail, rejoicing, dancing, shouting, contemplation, recitation, repentance, etc.)

You shouldn't be reading this line, unless you've completed the above assignment.

Finished with the diagram? Good.

Now, in dark bold letters, at the top of the page, print the word "PRAYER."

You have just put a title over your list. All the expressions you wrote down are various kinds of prayers.

The Specific And The General

To understand the biblical idea of prayer, we must understand that the word "prayer" is used two ways in the Bible. It is used, first of all, in the *specific* sense of "petition," "supplication," "presenting requests to God." When we pray in this specific sense, we say things like, "God, please bless my day. Bless my wife, my kids, my church. Help us to be able to afford the electric bill this month." Those are petitions for a specific need.

But "prayer" in the Bible is also used in a *general* sense, as a comprehensive term to describe the entire gamut of ways we express ourselves to God. Prayer in this general sense is what you have just diagrammed. All of those expressions you listed are forms of prayer.

Paul wrote, "And pray in the Spirit on all occasions with all kinds of prayers and requests" (Ephesians 6:18, NIV). How many kinds of prayers are there, Paul? All kinds of them, Paul

Diagram

says. And he exhorts us to employ all of them as we direct our hearts toward the Lord.

A Poised Spirit

Let me suggest a definition of prayer in this general sense. Prayer is: "A spirit poised toward God."

It is very important to understand that although my mind cannot always be focussed on the Lord, my spirit can be continually poised toward the Lord. When the Bible commands us to pray without ceasing, it means that we are to have our spirits poised toward the Lord every moment of every day. It's possible for our spirit to be praying when we're not aware of it — even while we're asleep.

Here's how it works. I'm driving along the highway and have become so preoccupied with the demands of driving that the Lord is not in my thoughts at all. But during a lull in the pace of the traffic, my mind wanders to something about the Lord. In that moment, my spirit immediately responds, and from within comes a quick "Thank You, Lord. I love You, Jesus." Why does my spirit respond like that? Because it has been poised toward the Lord all along. Although my mind can't focus on the things of God twenty-four hours a day, when my thoughts do come around to the Lord, my spirit is poised and ready to go.

Or perhaps you've experience the opposite effect. When your mind is brought around to focus on the Lord, you sense a coldness in your heart. A distance has come between the Lord and your spirit. You feel "out of it" spiritually. What's wrong? Your spirit lost its stance of being poised toward the Lord. Something caused your heart to become directed toward yourself, or the cares of the world.

Pray Without Ceasing

This dynamic becomes very obvious in congregational worship. It's Sunday morning, 10:00 a.m., and it's time for the worship service to begin. The worship leader introduces a song, and everyone begins to sing. For those whose spirits are poised toward God, they take off. It doesn't matter what song it is, if the song is fast or slow, if the instruments are in tune or off key, if the P.A. system is too loud or too quiet, these folks are ready to worship the Lord. They are immediately in the Spirit, and their joy and spiritual alertness is obvious.

And then you've got the other group. Mind you, they look ready for church, dressed up so nicely and all. But as the singing begins their minds are dwelling on thoughts like, "I wonder if Billy's going to make it to church today. I hope so, because if I can talk to him this morning it will save me a long-distance phone call." "What happened to that couple? Must have had a blow-up in the car on the way to the church. Tsk tsk." "Look at that outfit, will you! My, aren't we looking good today!"

It takes some people the first fifteen minutes of a worship service to get their spirit to even begin to move.

I'm going to tell you why some worship services take so long to get off the ground, or why some don't even fly at all. This is the reason behind every faltering worship service, every time. It is simply this: We have not been living out the word of Scripture that commands, "Pray without ceasing." Our spirits have not been poised toward the Lord.

Have you ever been in a worship service that ascended into heavenly places at the crack of the first song? Everybody's looking at the worship leader, thinking, "Wow, what an anointed worship leader!" Listen, it has nothing to do with the worship leader. Our spirits were poised toward the Lord, and we came ready to worship. The worship leader probably could have pulled out a funeral dirge and we would have exploded in praise. You get a group together whose spirits are poised toward God, and starting up a song is like putting a match to gasoline. The service will explode.

This is why one of the greatest challenges facing church leaders today is making disciples whose determination is to angle their spirits continually toward the Lord. He who has come to live a life of prayer understands that he can abide in the face of Christ even when tussling with his kids on the living room floor.

Prayer As A General Term

That "prayer" is sometimes used in a general way in the Bible to describe all the ways we express ourselves to God may be a new idea to some. So I would like to defend that thesis from some selected Scripture passages.

For starters, flip open to the second chapter of 1 Samuel. The first verse tells us that "Hannah prayed," and then Hannah's prayer is recorded for us. Hannah says, "My heart rejoices in the Lord" (v. 1) — she begins with praise. In the next verse she says, "No one is holy like the Lord, for there is none besides You, nor is there any rock like our God" (v.2) — that's a beautiful expression of worship. Now look at verse 4: "The bows of the mighty men are broken, and those who stumbled are girded with strength" — in this and the following verses Hannah breaks into something like "prophetic proclamation" as she extols the works of the Lord.

Here's my point: You will not find a single petition in Hannah's prayer. Not once does she ask God for anything. She praises, she worships, she extols God's greatness, she prophesies — and the Bible calls that "prayer." Why is there no petition in her prayer? Because prayer, in this general sense, is something far broader than petition only.

The Lord's Prayer

This thought is substantiated in the model prayer that Jesus gave His disciples. Jesus says, "When you pray, say: Our Father in heaven, hallowed be Your name" (Luke 11:2). Worship the Father when you pray, Jesus was telling them, because *worship is prayer.* Jesus also taught them to ask for their daily bread to be supplied, because *petition is prayer.* And finally, He taught them to conclude their prayer with these words: "For Yours is the kingdom and the power and the glory forever. Amen" (Matthew 6:13). Jesus taught them a closing chorus of praise, because *praise is prayer.* Jesus reinforced this concept that prayer has many expressions.

Look further with me, please, at a very short verse from David's writings: "The prayers of David the son of Jesse are ended" (Psalm 72:20). With these words, David is not concluding just Psalm 72, he is wrapping up an entire collection of psalms. (Notice that this verse ends "Book Two" of the Book of Psalms.) Examine the content of David's psalms, and you will discover a variety of expressions — petition, questioning, praise, adoration, prophecy, worship, weeping, exulting, cries for retribution and judgment on his enemies, etc. In conclusion, David uses one word to describe this wide assortment of expressions — "prayers."

I hope these texts validate sufficiently my thesis that "prayer" is sometimes used in a general, all-inclusive sense in the Bible.

Praise Prayers

This thesis is borne out in a very interesting way when we analyze the story of Paul and Silas in the Philippian jail. Paul and Silas angered the residents of Philippi for delivering a demonized woman, so after being severely beaten they were imprisoned with their feet in stocks. "But at midnight Paul and Silas were praying and singing hymns to God" (Acts 16:25). I discovered something very interesting from the construction of the original Greek wording of this Scripture: in the phrase "praying and singing," the conjunction "and" is entirely missing in the Greek. The phrase, literally, should read like this: "And towards midnight Paul and Silas praying were singing praises to God" (Berry's Interlinear Greek-English New Testament). Paul and Silas weren't doing two things (praying and singing), they were doing but one thing. They were praying. And the specific form of prayer they were employing was that of singing praises. They were singing "praise prayers."

God delivered Paul and Silas from that jail in a mighty way to demonstrate His pleasure in releasing His power when we give ourselves to praise prayers in our own midnight hour.

A Complete Expression

God wants us to practice the full orb of prayer expressions as we lift our souls to the Lord. If my prayer life is lacking any one of prayer's expressions, then it is not fully balanced and complete.

Some people have become regimented and rigid in their personal prayer life. "Five minutes for praise, five minutes for worship, five minutes for me, five minutes for my family, five minutes for my church, five minutes for my pastor, five minutes for my missionaries, five minutes for my country..." Their prayer life is so precisely preplanned that if one portion of their prayer time goes longer than it should, it throws their whole morning off.

God wants our time with Him to be a free-flowing expression of loving interaction. It may be that one morning you'll spend fifteen minutes in praise, and the next morning you'll spend thirty minutes in intercession. The Lord wants to direct your prayer time each day with a sense of ongoing freshness. But as you survey your prayer life over time, there should be a proper balance of the full gamut of all the expressions of prayer.

Praise And Worship In The New Testament

Now I want to take this principle and apply it in such a way that your heart will be encouraged. I have interacted with a lot of people who have studied the Bible quite extensively on the subjects of praise and worship, and they have frequently expressed this kind of sentiment: "I wish the New Testament would have more to say about praise and worship. It seems that we have to go to the Old Testament so much of the time to learn about praise and worship. Why doesn't the New Testament say more?" The foremost revelation on worship in the Bible is in John 4:23-24, and beyond that references to praise and worship in the New Testament seem to be rather few and far between.

Until now. We know that the New Testament has much to say about prayer. But if "prayer" is often used inclusively to describe praise and worship as well, then could we not suggest that "praise and worship" are discussed frequently in the New Testament under the banner of "prayer"? Let's check it out.

Acts 2:42 records the fourfold activity of the New Testament Church: "And they continued steadfastly in the apostles' doctrine and fellowship, in the breaking of bread, and in prayers." We see that one of "the big four" emphases was "prayers." Now, I can't imagine those first believers sitting around in circles, passing around prayer requests, praying for each others' needs, and then going home. They simply must have had times of exuberant praise and worship too! The word "prayers" means precisely that. We must see the New Testament Church in a new perspective — praise and worship was one of their primary activities.

Acts 6:4 gives the twofold focus of the apostles: "But we will give ourselves continually to prayer and to the ministry of the word." Again, "prayer" in the general sense is intended. The apostles were committed to prioritizing praise, worship, thanksgiving, intercession — all the forms of prayer — in their daily lives. I can hear Peter saying, "If the bulletin doesn't get finished, if I can't make all my hospital visits this week, if I can't return all my phone calls, this much I must do: Above all else I must have time in the face of Jesus, to worship Him, to adore Him, to cry out to Him, to be with Him." This was and continues to be an absolute priority for all church leaders.

Praise And Worship, And Jesus

Now we can raise another intriguing question: Why do the Gospels record so little of Jesus expressing Himself in praise and worship? If you've ever asked that question, I trust you will understand my thesis in this chapter, because Jesus' life was full of praise and worship. The Gospels record many times that Jesus prayed, and included in that term prayer are the expressions of praise and worship.

When the Gospel writers describe Jesus' prayer life, so often we find Him going off to a lonely place to pray in solitude. I have a fairly pictorial imagination, and so I immediately envision Jesus in the lonely desert places where He is praying. The picture my mind paints is my own creation, but let me describe it for you anyways, as you may have pictured something similar to this stereotypical image: Jesus is praying; His outer garment is bleach white (I don't understand why, since He's in a very dry, dusty desert part of the world, but nevertheless glistening white it is); He is seated, and His garment flows down and covers His feet; to His immediate left is a rock (how many can see the rock?); an almost-visible halo shimmers beautifully over His head; His hands are folded; and He is praying gently, just above a whisper. Do you get the image? And here's what Jesus is saying: "Father, bless my day. Help me to teach my disciples properly. Keep me from the evil one. Give me strength for today's challenges. Amen."

Beloved, I think that picture of Jesus praying is far from reality. When Jesus prayed, He did so much more than just present His requests and petitions. He also exulted with great joy as He delighted in His Father. He worshiped openly and unashamedly, lifting His voice in adoration and glory. When Jesus talked with His Father, sparks flew. There was such an effervescence in His relationship with the Father that the disciples badgered Him to teach them how to pray the same way.

Worship is based upon relationship. The more you know God, the deeper your worship will be. And no one knew the Father like Jesus. Jesus was the greatest worshiper of all time.

Jesus' Range Of Prayer Expressions

It is my personal conviction that one reason Jesus gravitated toward the lonely places to pray was because there He was able to "let it all hang out." There Jesus gave full vent to the passion of His heart and soul, employing the full spectrum of prayer's expressions. The writer of Hebrews captured this element in Jesus' prayer life: "...who, in the days of His flesh, when He had offered up prayers and supplications, with vehement cries and tears to Him who was able to save Him from death, and was heard because of His godly fear" (Hebrews 5:7). Jesus' prayer life included cries, tears, volume — a full orb of expression.

For our prayer lives to be complete and balanced, like Jesus we must employ the full gamut of prayers — from intercession to rejoicing, from weeping to laughing, from praise to worship, from dancing to kneeling, from shouting to silent meditation.

Somebody said, "Well, Jesus never danced!" Oh really? The Bible tells us that Jesus was anointed with a measure of joy greater than any of us have ever known (Hebrews 1:9). How do you think Jesus could have squelched all that joy? I can't imagine Him thinking, "I will not dance, I will not dance; no, I'm the Messiah, I can't lose it now; keep control of Yourself now, keep it together; You've got to repress the joy, they're watching You." Jesus didn't have the personality hang-ups that plague you and me; He was totally free to be Himself, totally free to express Himself candidly and authentically in the presence of His Father. Did Jesus ever dance? Perhaps your mental image needs to be touched up a bit.

Why would Jesus have a problem with dance as an expression of praise, and then turn around and command us to dance? "Rejoice in that day and leap for joy!" (Luke 6:23). Don't you understand that Jesus was the absolute embodiment of the Psalms?

Check It Out

This chapter would get too long if I took the time here to show how the word "prayer" in the New Testament opens up new shades of glorious truth when seen as a description of the full spectrum of multifarious expressions. But I would like to whet your appetite, so that you might go on such a study yourself.

Be sure to study out the Spirit's call to "be serious and watchful in your prayers" (1 Peter 4:7). Alertness is an important element in all forms of prayer. According to Colossians 4:2, thanksgiving should also accompany every prayer expression.

Take a close look at James 5:16, "The effective, fervent prayer of a righteous man avails much." Meditate in the delightful possibilities of these applications: "The effective, fervent *praise* of a righteous man avails much." "The effective, fervent *worship* of a righteous man avails much." "The effective, fervent *travail* of a righteous man avails much." The same applications can be made when looking at other translations. Barclay renders it, "The prayer of a good man, when it is set to work, is very powerful." Perhaps the best translation of this verse is the Revised Version: "The supplication of a righteous man availeth much in its working."

James 5:16 uses the Greek word "energeo," "to work," from which we get our word "energy." James is literally saying, "Your worship has energy with God. Your praises go to work." The book of Revelation teaches us that our prayers have an accumulative effect before God. According to Revelation 8:3-5, our prayers are collected in a censer, and God is described as turning at the appropriate time and commanding one of His angels, "Take that censer of prayers, and fling it back down to earth." When that censer hits the earth there's an explosion, thunderings and lightnings, and an earthquake. This is a picture of answered prayer. Even though your prayers don't appear to be having any energy with God, don't give up; keep on filling up your prayer censer in heaven. One day, years of cumulative prayer will be brought to bear in one moment upon the area of challenge, and a glorious victory will suddenly be manifest. What is a non-Christian husband to do when God knocks him over the head with twenty years' worth of a wife's faithful prayers?

I really don't have space here to pursue this any further. I sincerely hope you'll apply this "key" to a renewed understanding of prayer, praise, and worship in the New Testament.

Worship And Intercession

For too long we have separated prayer from praise, and worship from intercession. Something God is clearly doing in the body of Christ today is awakening a new understanding of how to use praise and worship to empower intercession.

God has used many ministries in recent years to call the body of Christ to prayer. Visit your local Christian bookstore, and look at all the prayer resources and accessories. They probably take up an entire aisle — books on prayer, workbooks on prayer, prayer journals, prayer calendars, prayer posters, prayer logs, cassettes on prayer, video teachings on prayer, prayer knee pads, prayer alarm clocks, prayer Post-Its. It's a prayer warrior's heaven.

God has also been calling the body of Christ to a renewed focus on praise and worship. Go ahead and check out the praise and worship aisle in your Christian bookstore. They've got books on worship, workbooks on worship, videos on worship, cassette teachings on worship, praise cassettes, praise CD's, worship lead sheets, praise T-shirts, praise tapes for kids, tambourines, praise batons, praise bazookas, praise bubblegum, paint-by-number praise & worship...

I'm being on the light side with it, but God has really changed the face of His Church in recent years through the voices that have called us to prayer and to praise. But one day the Spirit spoke clearly to my heart that there are not two sounds going forth (as though prayer and praise were distinct from each other). The trumpet is making but one sound. The Spirit is calling for one thing in this hour — men and women whose spirits are poised toward His face.

CHAPTER TWELVE

The Flavors Of Worship

As we are in His face, the Lord desires our worship to be diversified and full-orbed, according to the many expressions of worship laid forth in the Scriptures.

Worship is like a multifaceted jewel, shining in many directions simultaneously. There are many moods, elements, or what I would like to call "flavors" in worship. Just as a rainbow is complete only when all the colors are present, so the worship life of a local congregation is balanced only when the full diversity of flavors are present in the expressions of a church's corporate worship. In this chapter I would like to list eight flavors of worship that are necessary if we desire to expose worshipers to the full range of scriptural ways to express ourselves before God. These flavors of worship are also appropriate to our personal times with God.

Exaltation

With hands and hearts outstretched, we long to extol and magnify the greatness of the glorious God and Father of our Lord Jesus Christ. Songs such as "I Exalt Thee" and "Our God Is an Awesome God" give us the vocabulary to exalt His majesty. Exaltation is, in fact, the keynote of heaven's worship.

Some churches have yet to learn how to enter into corporate exaltation. When the clapping stops and the tambourines are put down, it's as though there's nothing left. Below the noise it's really very shallow. In such cases, a church needs to learn the depths of exaltation.

When we magnify the Lord, we aren't making the Lord any bigger than He already is. But think of a magnifying glass. When we magnify the Lord, we are gaining a sharper focus on who He is.

God isn't an egomaniac who sits up in heaven waiting for us to pump Him up. God is exalted above the heavens, whether or not we acknowledge that. He doesn't need to be exalted — we need to exalt Him. But you cannot exalt the Lord and maintain your "dignity". The only way to exalt the Lord is by humbling yourself.

Intimacy

Jesus came to romance us back to the heart of the Father. Worship is the language of love, the lavish affection of redeemed saints who have fallen "head-over-heels" in love with Jesus. Anointed songwriters have given us many songs that help us express our love to the Lord: "I Love You, Lord"; "In Moments Like These," and many more.

Perhaps the greatest indictment of the American Church is that we have left our first love. The antithesis of love isn't hate, it's apathy. Living in the comforts of our society, I find I must continually rouse myself from the encroaching tentacles of apathy and lethargy. We're called to be "red hot" in our love for Christ, to walk among the "fiery stones" of the immediate presence of God in our ministry to the Most High (see Ezekiel 28:14). Have you fallen in love with Jesus all over again today?

Although I relish the sweetness of intimacy with Jesus, let me point out that it's only one of eight flavors. Some groups have focussed on sweet songs of intimacy almost to the exclusion of any other flavor. Intimacy gains fuller meaning when positioned next to some of the other necessary flavors of worship, such as the next one — celebration.

Celebration

It's party time, Church! Pull out the stops and celebrate the risen Savior! Here I think of songs like "Celebrate Jesus" and "In Him We Live and Move and Have Our Being." Praise is "raising a big flap" about a great God. As I heard one brother say, praise is "going bananas" over Jesus.

And yet some churches don't know how to celebrate. Maybe the greatness of their salvation hasn't impacted them yet. Paul prayed that "the eyes of your understanding being enlightened; that you may know what is the hope of His calling, what are the riches of the glory of His inheritance in the saints, and what is the exceeding greatness of His power toward us who believe, according to the working of His mighty power" (Ephesians 1:18-19). Get that into your spirit and you'll celebrate!

Somebody said, "Let's cool it a little. We don't want to scare off those who might not understand." Listen, folks: As wickedness increases all around us, we need the strength that comes from rejoicing in the Lord. Brother, you better learn how to celebrate — in these last days it's going to become a matter of survival.

And now for a word of balance. Worshipers need to be sensitive to "corporate dynamics" when in the congregation. There's a time for celebration, and also a time for quiet reverence. Don't celebrate in such a way that you draw attention from the Lord to yourself. Learn to party with the best of them, and also learn to clamp it down when the mood of the service changes.

Proclamation

This may be one of the most misunderstood flavors of worship. In proclamation, we are declaring the greatness and goodness of God in the hearing of a third party. Songs such as "Great Is the Lord" and "What a Mighty God We Serve" are like sung announcements, proclaiming to anyone within earshot what we think about Jesus. Incredible power is released in a service simply in the proclamation of the name of the Lord. When we sing songs like, "I Am the God That Healeth Thee," our singing transcends the music and becomes an enforcement of kingdom dominion.

Psalm 66:8 admonishes, "Let the sound of His praise be *heard*." It's not praise until it's verbalized. It wasn't that long ago that we were potty training our youngest child Michael.

If we had just thought nice thoughts when he produced on the potty, we would have gotten nowhere. You should have heard us — we clapped, we hooted, we cheered. Now that's praise!

Somebody once said, "Let's stop singing songs about Jesus, and sing songs to Jesus." But it's equally scriptural to sing about Jesus. Paul exhorts us to "Speak to one another with psalms, hymns and spiritual songs" (Ephesians 5:19). The Israelites daily recited to one another this declaration about the Lord: "The Lord is good, and His mercy endures forever."

With so many new songs being written and made available to the Church today, it is very important what songs we select to sing in the congregation. The songs we select determine what truths we will declare about the Lord. In the final analysis, the things we say about the Lord in our songs become those things that are best remembered and embraced by both adults and children.

With some songs it's inappropriate to shut your eyes. Try this sometime: Open your eyes, turn to someone, and sing to them the high praises of God!

Warfare

The Bible calls us an army, and a balanced menu of worship must include the flavor of warfare. Songs like "The Battle Belongs to the Lord" and "I Hear the Sound of the Army of the Lord" help rouse the Church to a place of battle readiness.

Have you noticed that Christian T-shirts for teens are getting more and more radical? I think youth leaders understand something: As wickedness becomes more blatant and prevalent, our kids need a militancy to survive. The devil's turning up the heat because he knows his time is short, so the Church that will crush him in this hour must also turn up the heat.

Yes, there can be an over-emphasis here too. Warfare is only one of eight flavors. It's possible to become a lopsided, one-issue church. Incessant warfare every Sunday morning is wearisome. But make no mistake, there is a renewed emphasis of the Holy Spirit upon warfare in worship.

Prophetic

Full-orbed worship must include a prophetic flavor. There comes a time in a service when the spirit of worship actually kindles and sparks the flow of prophetic utterances in a congregation.

Just as the melodious harp soothed Elisha's indignation and stirred up his prophetic gifting (see 2 Kings 3:1-20), so the ministry of anointed musicians can inspire the spirit of prophecy among God's people.

A worship service gives us the tremendous satisfaction of expressing our affections to God. And then the pastor says, "You may be seated." I can visualize God sitting on the edge of His throne, with something on the tip of His tongue, but lo, it's time for the announcements. He didn't gain the satisfaction of also sharing His heart with us. But that's the essence of prophetic worship: two-way communication.

A tremendous way to encourage the prophetic flavor is through the use of "spiritual songs" (Colossians 3:16). By playing simple, repetitive chord progressions, musicians can provide the necessary atmosphere for spontaneous, improvised, straight-from-the-heart songs that carry the prophetic impetus of the Spirit.

Entreaty

God is calling us to broaden our worship to include the flavors of petition and intercession. The Spirit has inspired many songs in this hour that are in fact prayers of entreaty, some examples being "Shine Jesus Shine," "Lord, Have Mercy on Us," and "Change My Heart O God."

Jesus declared, "My house will be called a house of prayer" (Matthew 21:13), and yet far too few of our worship services actually include an element of supplication or intercession. Think about it — when your church gathers, do you become actively involved in corporate prayer?

Special Occasion

"Special occasion" is the term I've chosen for the eighth flavor, for lack of a better one I suppose. Here I'm talking about the kinds of songs we sing at special times of the year such as Christmas, Easter, or Thanksgiving.

I would also lump under this heading the kinds of songs we sing during altar calls — songs of consecration like "I Have Decided to Follow Jesus."

The Centrality Of All Worship: Jesus

As you review the eight flavors that comprise a balanced menu of worship for local churches, I'd like to remind you that the central focus of all worship is the Lord Jesus. He is the "hub" around which all else turns.

I have been asked, "What do you think is the 'now' thing God is saying to the Body of Christ in the area of worship?" At the risk of sounding simplistic I would have to say, "Jesus, Jesus, Jesus." He is the Alpha and Omega of all worship. Move away from focussing on Jesus and you're off center.

May the Lord enable us as we spend time in worship, to be open to and expressive of all the flavors of worship, in proper balance, with the face of our Lord Jesus Himself being our focus at all times. Amen.

Part Four:

Into His Image

CHAPTER THIRTEEN

Adopting A Godly Self-Image

For I say, through the grace given to me, to everyone who is among you, not to think of himself more highly than he ought to think, but to think soberly, as God has dealt to each one a measure of faith. (Romans 12:3)

This is perhaps the clearest instruction in the entire Bible, in a single verse, on how we should view ourselves. The word "soberly" means "sane, moderate, serious, restrained, disciplined, self-controlled, to be of sound mind." This Scripture exhorts us, then, to think of ourselves properly, moderately, in a well-balanced, healthy way. The verse carries a twofold caution, that we not think too highly of ourselves (pride), and that we not think too disparagingly of ourselves (insecurity).

Nobody Loves Me, Everybody Hates Me

People today have a high self-awareness. And so we have a plethora of fitness centers, health foods, face-lifts, tummy tucks, liposuction, diets, exercise bikes, etc. Americans are searching religiously for a positive self-image.

One woman gets up in the morning, walks over to the mirror and says, "Good morning, Ugly." We don't like our weight, our complexion, or the proportions of our physical features. We are dissatisfied with our personality, we wish we had a higher I.Q., and we don't make enough money to buy the house we want.

Even people who have much are dissatisfied. A former Miss

America, when asked by her husband what she would change if she could, immediately listed several physical features with which she was unhappy. Whether real or imagined, many people struggle with feelings of inferiority.

Some people, however, try to cope with far more serious challenges. Millions carry the scars of severe mental, emotional, sexual, or physical abuse. Many people struggle to block out the haunting words that have seemed to seal their fate: "You're just like your father." "Why are you so stupid?" "You're never going to amount to anything."

Others just wish they had parents. But instead they were raised in foster homes, getting shuffled from one guardian to another. Or perhaps their parents divorced, leaving a gaping emotional wound that is still tender. We live in the age of "the walking wounded." No one can argue that the problem is very real and very overwhelming. The majority of people are struggling to some degree with their self-image.

The Diagnosis

The world has given us its diagnosis. "The problem," the psychiatrists tell us, "is that you have low self-esteem." So what can be done about that? We need to build up our self-image, we're told, by coming to believe how wonderful we are.

"You have a divine spark in you!"

"You are wonderful — just believe in yourself."

"You can make your own world."

"Reach for the top. You've got what it takes."

And so counselors and therapists are working overtime to indoctrinate their patients in the tenets of humanism. With only one problem — it's not working.

Psychology Versus Theology

The explosion of psychiatry and psychology in this century has given rise to a very heated and controversial debate within the Church. Some Christian leaders see the advances, research, and discoveries of psychology as actually serving the purposes of the Church, whereas others see them as running countercurrent to the teachings of the Bible.

I will be quoting several outstanding Christian leaders in

this chapter, some with whom I agree, and others with whom I disagree on this subject. I honor each of their ministries, and do not mention their names in order to detract in any way from the validity of their ministries. But I mention their names in order to help you understand the intensity of the controversy in the Body of Christ.

Bill Gothard has said, "The major problem of young people in this nation is poor self-image." James Dobson, a vocal proponent of this camp, writes, "Of all the problems women have, number one on the list, causing depression, causing loneliness and emptiness, is low self-esteem." Dr. Dobson, in his book *Hide Or Seek*, goes on to say:

> *In a real sense, the health of an entire society depends on the ease with which its individual members can gain personal acceptance. Thus, whenever the keys to self-esteem are seemingly out of reach for a large percentage of the people, as in twentieth-century America, then widespread "mental illness", neuroticism, hatred, alcoholism, drug abuse, violence, and social disorder will certainly occur. Personal worth is not something human beings are free to take or leave. We must have it, and when it is unattainable, everybody suffers.*

Robert Schuller, who believes that theologians and psychologists need to learn from each other, has suggested that some of us need to rework our theology in order to integrate some of the scientific discoveries of psychologists.

It's as though God in heaven, while watching Freud at work, slapped His forehead and cried, "I should have thought of that! Too bad I didn't think to include that in the Bible."

A fundamental premise of my position in this chapter is that God has not been educated by the discoveries of psychiatrists. God has placed in His revealed word, the Bible, everything that we need to know for living godly lives in Christ Jesus (2 Peter 1:3). Psychology must not shape our understanding of the Bible; the Bible must judge every supposition of psychology.

Psychology is the study of the old man. The best that

psychologists can do is analyze, diagnose, and assign labels. "You're manic depressive." "You're schizophrenic." They might be able to evaluate your problem and help you understand why you are the way you are, but they're relatively incapable of helping you deal with the root causes of your problems or of bringing you to ultimate healing. At best they can help you cope.

Love Thyself

There is a common teaching in the Church today that we are to love ourselves. If we lack self-love, they say, then we should give ourselves diligently to increasing our love for ourselves.

The basis for this teaching comes most frequently from a false interpretation of Mark 12:28-31:

> *Then one of the scribes came, and having heard them reasoning together, perceiving that He had answered them well, asked Him, "Which is the first commandment of all?" Jesus answered him, "The first of all the commandments is: 'Hear, O Israel, the LORD our God, the LORD is one. And you shall love the LORD your God with all your heart, with all your soul, with all your mind, and with all your strength.' This is the first commandment. And the second, like it, is this: 'You shall love your neighbor as yourself.' There is no other commandment greater than these."*

The reasoning goes like this: In order to love my neighbor, I must first love myself. If I don't love myself, I am incapable of loving my neighbor properly. Furthermore, according to Christian author Walter Trobisch, there is in man no inborn self-love. Self-love is either acquired or it is non-existent. Therefore, if I am to fulfill Jesus' mandate to love my neighbor, I must first of all commit myself energetically to loving myself. Self-love becomes a prerequisite for serving our neighbor. As one leader expressed it, "Loving ourselves is a command ranking in importance next to loving God."

The problem with this teaching is that it originated with

Friedrich Nietzche (father of the "God is dead" philosophy), and then was advanced by psychologist Erik Fromm.

I invite you to take another look at the teaching of Jesus in this passage. Jesus wasn't commanding self-love, He was saying, "You already do love yourself. You're born with it. Now love your neighbor in the same way." I had the privilege of watching my three children come into the world. The first thing a newborn baby does is bawl, and you know what the baby is thinking, "I'm here! I'm cold! I'm hungry! I don't like what you're doing to me!" From the moment of our birth we are consumed with self-love.

Paul confirmed this when he wrote, "For no one ever hated his own flesh" (Ephesians 5:29). Be honest and admit, "I love myself."

"Is it sinful to love myself?" No. It's self-love that stimulates you to dress yourself, feed yourself, brush your teeth, and put on deodorant. All of us are very thankful you love yourself! But what is sinful is when you feed that self-love. Instead of using self-love to focus on ourselves, Jesus has instructed us to divert that energy outward into the love of others. "...and they did not love their lives to the death" (Revelation 12:11).

Somebody might say, "Oh, but I do hate myself! Look at my awful face! Look at those horrible hips! I can't stand myself!" Actually, you love yourself. You love yourself very much. You love yourself so much that you're all upset over the circumstances that have enveloped you. If you really hate yourself, then why are you so upset by your circumstances? If you hated yourself, you'd be glad you're ugly!

Somebody else might argue, "But how about people who commit suicide? Surely they must hate themselves if they're willing to kill themselves." They may hate their circumstances, or they may hate how people respond to them, but they love themselves. They love themselves so much that they want to free themselves from the emotional trauma of everyday living. Suicide is the ultimate statement of self-love.

When the apostle Paul wrote Timothy, he told Timothy that things would get real bad in the last days. To emphasize how bad it would get, Paul began his description of the last days with this warning, "For men will be lovers of themselves"

(2 Timothy 3:2). The self-love movement of this generation is yet another evidence that we are living in the last of the last days.

Self-Forgiveness

Another teaching that is commonly heard in Christian circles today is the idea that sometimes we need to forgive ourselves. We're told that some people have not found a complete spiritual release because they haven't been able to forgive themselves for their past sins.

But not once does the Bible ever direct us to forgive ourselves. It's simply not a scriptural concept. The Bible seems to indicate that the only forgiveness I really need is God's forgiveness, or the forgiveness of a brother or sister.

People who say they can't forgive themselves are harboring nothing short of the sin of pride. They're saying, "I can't believe I did that! What a dumb thing to do! I know I'm better than that. I can't get over the fact that I did that, especially considering that I'm capable of so much better."

Listen, my friend: You're capable of committing the worst sin imaginable. It's only by God's grace that you didn't do something worse. Acknowledge the wickedness of your heart, recognize that God's mercy kept you from doing something worse, and come to God for His forgiveness. If you will receive the cleansing power of the blood of Jesus, your sins will be washed away for eternity, and you will be completely free to stand in His presence!

Repentance

One reason some psychologists hate the gospel is because the message of repentance is so radically opposed to their teachings. True repentance *destroys* your self-image. Repentance acknowledges what God says about us, and in utter brokenness cries out, "I am nothing! I am a foolish sinner. Oh God, please help me!" Jesus came for the purpose of devastating your self-image. He wants you to recognize your absolute poverty, so that He can make you into an entirely new person with a whole new lease on life.

You can't repent properly until you see yourself as God

sees you. The big question is, "How does God see me?" Some Christian leaders are answering that question like this: "Every human being is a person of great worth and dignity." "We are something beautiful that God has done. We are something exquisite that He has planned." "The human being is a glorious, dignified creature with infinite value." "God wants us to see ourselves as His gift to the world."

In contrast, look at what the Bible says about us:

> *Then the LORD saw that the wickedness of man was great in the earth, and that every intent of the thoughts of his heart was only evil continually.* (Genesis 6:5)

> *The LORD looks down from heaven upon the children of men, to see if there are any who understand, who seek God. They have all turned aside, they have together become corrupt; there is none who does good, no, not one.* (Psalm 14:2-3)

> *The heart is deceitful above all things, and desperately wicked; who can know it?* (Jeremiah 17:9)

> *And you He made alive, who were dead in trespasses and sins, in which you once walked according to the course of this world, according to the prince of the power of the air, the spirit who now works in the sons of disobedience, among whom also we all once conducted ourselves in the lusts of our flesh, fulfilling the desires of the flesh and of the mind, and were by nature children of wrath, just as the others.* (Ephesians 2:1-3)

It is false teaching that says Christ died for us because of our great value. God didn't send His Son to earth because He couldn't help Himself. No, the cross is an expression of the infinite grace and mercy of our Father, who sent His Son to die for us even while we were still sinners (Romans 5:8). God redeemed us so that we mi   >e a showcase of His grace (Ephesians 2:6-7). Luther saiu, God does not love us because we're valuable; we're valuable because God loves us."

What has made us valuable to God is Christ's sacrifice. We are as valuable to God as the price He paid for us. As incredible as it sounds, we are God's reward for the price of His Son. That's why the Moravians carried this motto, "To gain for the Lamb the reward of His sacrifice."

From God's Perspective

We don't like to think of ourselves as that utterly sinful, but true repentance agrees with God's assessment of our condition. Without God's objective evaluation, we would have no idea as to our true depravity.

To illustrate, have you ever stayed inside a small room or office for an extended period of time? The air in the room seems normal to you, but when somebody comes into the room from the outside, they turn up their nose and say, "It's stuffy in here!" Because of your confinement, you were unaware of the stuffy odor of your room. Similarly, man reeks with sin, but he's too accustomed to it to realize the stench in which he's living. We need God to come from without, and say to us, "Your sin stinks."

Using Biblical Language

When diagnosing someone's problem, I would like to impress upon you the importance of using biblical language. Find a way to describe their condition with biblical terminology. When you try to describe someone's condition with non-biblical language you begin to walk on very thin ice.

It's dangerous to say to someone, "Your problem is low self-esteem," because the term "low self-esteem" is not found anywhere in the Bible. Yet we know that people struggle with very real problems. So if the problem is not "low self-esteem," then what is it?

Scripturally, the problem is pride and unbelief. Obviously we need wisdom in how to present that message to someone, but in the final analysis, the believer with a poor self-image is actually struggling with pride and unbelief.

Pride

Pride is a human malady. Most people have a natural tendency to think more of themselves than they should. I will use just three examples to illustrate.

- Two doctors studied over 200 criminals, and discovered that each criminal thought of himself as a basically good person, even when planning a crime.
- In one study, 94% of college faculty rated their teaching abilities as "above average." I don't know what an average teacher is, but 94% of them considered themselves better than that.
- *TIME* Magazine (Feb. 5, 1990) reported on a math test given to thirteen-year-olds from six countries. The students from South Korea got the best scores, and the Americans got the worst. At the same time they were asked to evaluate how good they were at mathematics. The Koreans had the fewest students who felt they were good at math, and the Americans had the greatest percentage of students who felt they were good at math. Typical to prideful human nature, the worst math students thought they were the best.

Unbelief

Perhaps the most universal sin among Christians is this: We don't believe what God says about us. We've had more faith in our inabilities than in Christ's abilities through us. If we truly believed the testimony of Scripture regarding what Christ has done in us, we wouldn't struggle for another moment with anything remotely resembling low self-esteem.

God wants us to view ourselves correctly, as He sees us. To come to that proper self-perspective involves two basic but important scriptural concepts: repentance and faith. In repentance, I renounce my pride and unbelief. In faith, I embrace the full provision of redemption through Christ.

Christ In You

Here's the gospel message: God kills off your "old man," and then starts all over by birthing you anew with incorruptible seed (1 Peter 1:23). Now you have a whole new basis for looking at yourself. Now you're a child of God!

A healthy, godly self-image is based upon Colossians 1:27, "To them God willed to make known what are the riches of the glory of this mystery among the Gentiles: which is *Christ in you,* the hope of glory." Everything we understand about ourselves is now predicated upon this most glorious truth, that Christ lives within us.

Another important Scripture in coming to a godly self-image is 2 Corinthians 4:7, "But we have this treasure in earthen vessels, that the excellence of the power may be of God and not of us." Go ahead and say this out loud: "I am a jar — but I have a treasure!" I am only a container. If I look at the container, I will be very unimpressed. But look at what is being contained in the jar — Christ! Get a handle on this, beloved, and "low self-esteem" is gone forever. The Christian views himself as someone who embodies the person of Jesus Christ wherever he goes. Depression, hit the road!

Put Down The Put-Downs

Now that I carry Christ, I must be very careful not to disparage what God has done in me. Paul wrote, "For I know that in me (that is, in my flesh) nothing good dwells" (Romans 7:18). Paul recognized that the jar itself was nothing, but he had to clarify himself in this statement because something good did in fact dwell in him — Christ.

The Lord warned me about this tendency we have to disparage and belittle who we are. I was reading in the book of Acts about Peter's vision at noontime on the roof. God revealed to Peter a cluster of animals that were ceremonially unclean according to the Law, and said to him, "Rise, Peter; kill and eat."

Peter replied, "No, Lord, I've never eaten an unclean animal."

And this was God's response to Peter: *"What God has cleansed you must not call common"* (Acts 10:15).

You must hear this, dear believer: Never demean or call unclean the person who has been cleansed by God. Including yourself. "Oh, I'm nothing." That was once true. But now you are a child of God, with Christ Jesus Himself residing within you. Nothing? Hardly.

"I'm just a sinner." You're not *just* a sinner; you're a sinner that has been transformed by the almighty power of Christ's cross into a glorious saint of God!

"But I have an abusive, alcoholic father. I'll never change." Are you telling me that God is an alcoholic? You have a new Father, and an entire new lease on life! When the accuser whispers in your ear, "I can't do anything for God," then declare the truth of God's word about yourself: "I can do all things through Christ who strengthens me." Every facet of your existence has been revolutionized by Christ's presence within you. You can never view yourself the same again.

Affirming Our Children

Christian family counselors are telling us we need to instill self-love into our children so that they'll grow up secure and well-adjusted. So we lie to our kids: "You can do anything you want to do. The sky's the limit, son. Go for the gold!" Too often our attempts to encourage our children are in fact causing them to place their confidence in the flesh.

Christian parents have a responsibility to direct their children's confidence toward the Lord. We need to tell them, "Son, you can do everything that Christ calls you to do, because Philippians 4:13 says that when we are serving God in His will and way, He gives us the strength to fulfill His will."

Say to your daughter, "Sweetheart, you need to understand that there is nothing good in your flesh. If you try to serve God in your own strength you will be a miserable failure. If Jesus could do nothing apart from His Father, then understand that you need God desperately every moment of every day. If you allow His grace and strength to flow through your life, you will do mighty exploits for the Kingdom of God."

It is important to encourage our children, but we must encourage them in what God is doing in their lives. Instead of just praising their intellect or their good looks, point to the things that God is doing in and through them. "I see the Lord really helping you to become more caring toward your brother." "I am so thankful to the Lord for helping you get good grades this term." In this way, we encourage our children and give praise to God.

Rejecting Rejection

Many children suffer from rejection, or from insufficient nurturing in their childhood years. But God has purposed to use such tragedies to further His kingdom among us. Let me illustrate this with a simple allegory.

The little fish was thrown back into the water by the fisherman because he was too small. But the little fish was overcome with feelings of rejection — especially since his older brother was accepted by the fisherman. What the little fish didn't realize is that he was much better off with the rejection than with the acceptance.

Similarly, God makes rejection a positive thing in our lives. He uses it to cut through our false sense of security, and show us our true need. Many well-adjusted, accepted, affirmed people are on their way to hell. But on the other hand, many people who have been deeply wounded by rejection have turned to the healing power of Jesus Christ, and now enjoy the eternal acceptance of the Father.

Now, because of the rejection you've known, the Lord will use you in a unique way to reach certain people that others wouldn't be able to reach. "The sacrifices of God are a broken spirit" (Psalm 51:17). If you will offer your broken heart to God, He will accept the incense of your worship, and in turn use your brokenness to minister wholeness to others.

Comparisons

Christians are easily tempted to compare themselves with other Christians. Using the terminology of Jesus' parable in Matthew 25:14-30, the two-talent guy looks at the one-talent guy and feels a little bit superior. But then the two-talent guy looks at the five-talent guy, and suddenly feels very inferior. As long as we allow ourselves to compare ourselves with others, we will have constant struggles with our self-image. We'll be torn between the extremes of pride and insecurity. The

Scriptures constantly urge us to keep our focus on Jesus.

Look at yourself and you'll see an earthen vessel and get depressed. Look at other people and you'll either get arrogant or discouraged. Look at Jesus and you'll flourish in the radiance of His face.

Reflecting His Glory

I'd like to close this chapter with a Scripture that describes what God is doing in those who behold His face.

> *And we, who with unveiled faces all reflect the Lord's glory, are being transformed into His likeness with ever-increasing glory, which comes from the Lord, who is the Spirit.* (2 Corinthians 3:18, NIV)

As we are in His presence, beholding His face and reflecting His glory, this Scripture assures us that we're being changed more and more into the likeness of Christ.

One day the bathroom mirror went to visit the shrink. "Come, relax in this recliner," the psychiatrist said to the mirror. "Now what seems to be the problem?"

"I feel so yucky about myself," the bathroom mirror moaned.

"Oh really? Now why would you feel like that?"

"Well, nobody appreciates me for who I am," the mirror began. "Everybody just uses me. When they come into the bathroom, people don't even notice me. All they do is gape at themselves. And then when they run the shower, I get all steamed up. Then their hair sticks to me. They get their grubby fingerprints on me. And when they brush their teeth, it spatters all over me."

"I think I see your problem," the psychiatrist interrupted. "Your problem is, you have a poor self-image."

And with that diagnosis, the psychiatrist proceeded to build up the mirror's self-image. "You really are a wonderful mirror, you know. You have magnificently clear glass. And your border — my, I haven't seen a finer border on a mirror. What with your bevelled corners and all, why, you're one of the finest bathroom mirrors they make."

Stop. I'm interrupting this illustration. Would you agree

that this is a ludicrous illustration? It's obvious why. It's because a mirror wasn't made to have a self-image. A mirror was made to reflect the image of another.

Christians who are trying to establish a healthy self-image are missing the point altogether. They're focussing on who they are in Christ, rather than on who Christ is in them. Instead, get caught up in reflecting the glory of the Lord. Behold the beauty of His majesty and glory. And as you give yourself to beholding His face, you won't have any more problems with your self-image. You'll forget about yourself, and will be completely consumed with the beauty of His face.

> *As for me, I will see Your face in righteousness; I shall be satisfied when I awake in Your likeness.* (Psalm 17:15)

CHAPTER FOURTEEN

Spiritual Fatherhood

In this final chapter, I would like to discuss where I believe the Church is at today in the processes of God. There is a generation of young leaders that God is grooming for spiritual fatherhood.

Three Stages Of Maturity

> I write to you, little children, because your sins are forgiven you for His name's sake. 13 I write to you, fathers, because you have known Him who is from the beginning. I write to you, young men, because you have overcome the wicked one. I write to you, little children, because you have known the Father. 14 I have written to you, fathers, because you have known Him who is from the beginning. I have written to you, young men, because you are strong, and the word of God abides in you, and you have overcome the wicked one. (1 John 2:12-14)

The apostle John lays out for us what could be described as three stages of spiritual maturity.

Spiritual Childhood

The beginning level of spiritual maturity is "spiritual childhood". John addresses the "little children" and describes them in the following ways:

- They know that their sins are forgiven (v.12). These young believers know what the blood of Jesus has accomplished for them. They know what it means to live free from guilt and condemnation, and they revel in the acceptance of God. It is unfortunate that so many believers struggle for years to find this place of assurance, when we consider that it is only a "childhood" attainment in Christ.
- Spiritual children have come to know God as Father (v.13). Fathers provide three basic things for their children: protection, provision, and identity.
  1. Protection: Spiritual children have come to trust in the protective care of their loving Father. They have learned to rest securely in His loving embrace.
  2. Provision: Spiritual children can believe God for their daily bread. They have learned spiritual principles of stewardship, and know what it means to watch God supply their needs.
  3. Identity: In nations that follow our Judeo-Christian heritage, children take on the surname of their father. And it is the emotional nurturing of his or her father that best enables a child toward a healthy sexual identity and proper self-image. Spiritual children, similarly, have learned that the fullness of their new identity is in Christ, and not in themselves. They know who they are in Christ, and who Christ is in them.

Spiritual Adulthood

John moves on from there to the next phase of spiritual maturity, which could be termed "spiritual adolescence" or "spiritual adulthood." Let's look at how the apostle describes these young adults in Christ:

- These spiritual "young men" have overcome the wicked one (v.13). They have gained victory over temptation. They understand what the armor of God is all about, and they equip themselves daily with their armor. They know about spiritual warfare; they have engaged the enemy — they're giant killers.

- These young adults are "strong" (v.14). They are full of faith and of the Holy Spirit. They are bold in their confession, and they can believe God for great exploits. They are visionary leaders, and their lives are stable and exemplary.
- The word of God abides in them (v.14). These young men have studied the word, and they know the Scriptures. They're able to teach, and they are preachers of the gospel. They have solid understanding of the great themes of redemption: grace, the cross, the blood, the name of Jesus, the Holy Spirit, holiness, sanctification, healing, deliverance, repentance, spiritual gifts, the laying on of hands, etc. Because of their knowledge, they are able to refute error and expose false teaching.

As I considered how the apostle describes these spiritual "young men," I realized that in my mind I had come to conceive of that level of attainment as the height of spiritual growth. To be strong in spiritual warfare and to be a student of the word has been considered by many of us the ultimate attainment. It is sad to acknowledge that many believers never grow to this spiritual level, and it is not even the highest plane of maturity.

Spiritual Fatherhood

The last stage of spiritual growth could be called "spiritual fatherhood." John writes to the "fathers" in the Church, and he says only one thing to describe these spiritual parents: "you have known Him who is from the beginning" (vv.13-14).

Your first response when you read that is, "Big deal." It was more exciting at the childhood stage, or the young adult stage. Taking on the devil, applying the blood, teaching and preaching the word, now *this* is kingdom action! In contrast, there's something almost bland about "knowing Him who is from the beginning."

But spiritual fathers have come to a place of knowing God in His eternal attributes — His infinity, His sovereignty, His omniscience, His omnipotence, His greatness beyond anything we can comprehend. Spiritual fathers have come to the place where they truly know God.

The Trauma Of Maturing

Every level of maturity is achieved through pain. You got saved in the first place because of pain. In His grace, God showed you your great need, and in the desperation of your soul you turned to Him. In the same way, we move into each phase of spiritual growth through pain.

How many can remember that it was tough at times to be a kid? But it was even tougher to be a teenager. And yet every parent knows that nothing compares to the challenge of raising offspring. Maturity is great, but it is gained through difficulty, hardship, turmoil, and pain.

Spiritual Darkness

One of the painful tools God uses to bring "young men" into "spiritual fatherhood" is "spiritual darkness." Winkie Pratney has distinguished this process by noting that there are four kinds of darkness in the Bible: 1) There is the darkness of sin (John 3:19). 2) There is the darkness of ignorance (1 John 1:5). 3) Demonic powers are referred to in Scripture as "the powers of darkness" (Acts 26:18; Ephesians 6:12; Colossians 1:13). 4) Finally, there is a darkness that comes from God (Isaiah 50:10-11).

It should not surprise you that God sends darkness to His children. He is described as inhabiting darkness. On the mountain, Moses approached "the thick darkness where God was" (Deuteronomy 5:22). Pratney has defined this darkness as, above all, "a withdrawn sense of the presence of God." Not that God withdraws from us, but our perception is that He has withdrawn.

In actuality, when troubles confront us He is with us in a very real way. "God is our refuge and strength, a very present help in trouble" (Psalm 46:1). Jesus has promised to presence Himself in certain specific circumstances: He presences Himself when two or three gather together in His name (Matthew 18:20); He presences Himself in the midst of praises (Psalm 22:3); but Psalm 46:1 also promises that He presences Himself with those who are in trouble.

If you're in trouble, be assured of this: *Jesus is with you!* Darkness may seem to surround you and God may seem to have deserted you, but you cannot believe what you see right now, you must walk by what you cannot see. Hear the force of His promise, "Because he has loved Me...I will be with him in trouble" (Psalm 91:14-15). Although you feel as though God has forsaken you, He is with you — if it were possible — even more now than ever.

> *Who among you fears the LORD? Who obeys the voice of His Servant? Who walks in darkness and has no light? Let him trust in the name of the LORD and rely upon his God. 11 Look, all you who kindle a fire, who encircle yourselves with sparks: Walk in the light of your fire and in the sparks you have kindled — This you shall have from My hand: You shall lie down in torment.* (Isaiah 50:10-11)

This passage describes a man who fears the Lord, who obeys the voice of Jesus, who is a servant of God, and yet is walking in darkness. Some of you who are reading this are living in that place right now, but some of you are struggling to understand what I'm saying because you've never yet had a season of darkness like this hit your life. That's okay, enjoy your season of light. But take notes, and underline those statements that stand out to you, because seasons of darkness eventually will come to every man and woman of God who is serious about growing in the grace of God. It is in the dark seasons that we learn a greater dimension of trust and reliance upon God.

David Wilkerson made this great statement in one of his newsletters: "One reason some of you aren't hearing the voice of God is because He isn't talking to you right now." Sometimes we don't hear Him because of something we're doing wrong (sin, compromise, etc.); sometimes we don't hear Him because of something right we're not doing (self-discipline, self-denial, etc.); and sometimes we don't hear Him because He is purposefully withholding Himself for a season. God uses silence as one of His specialty tools to cultivate godliness within us.

Another reason we don't hear God is because He's not saying what we want to hear. We want Him to talk about our darkness, to explain it, and to tell us when it will lift. But He wants to talk about something else. We would do better to cock our ears, and just listen to what He wants to say. Even though this may be your season of darkness, you should be keeping a journal; in retrospect you'll be amazed at how much God was speaking to you.

Making Your Own Light

The temptation, when you can't see anything, is to take matters into your own hands and make your own light (verse 11). If God's not showing you the next step to take, you try to come up with a pathway or solution on your own. But Isaiah cautions us, "If God does not bring you light, you must not make your own." He led you into this darkness, and you must trust that He will bring you out. One creative word brought the universe into existence, and all you need is one word that proceeds from the mouth of God. Don't concoct a word of your own; wait for Him to bring it to you.

You will learn some things in darkness. You will discover that certain foundation stones which you thought were unshakable in your life are now shaken to the core. For example, it was during my darkness that I came to realize I was questioning my fundamental trust in God. Previous to the darkness, if there was one thing that I was sure was strongly intact in my life, it was trust. "This much I know, I trust God." Then the darkness hit. It was as though I had to learn all over again what it meant to trust.

In the dark season, everything that can be shaken will be shaken. But if you can come out of the darkness with something intact, then it's yours to keep! You will have learned what it means to trust Him when everything screams that God has been unfaithful to you.

You will be emptied of every notion of your own strength, and will develop a profoundly deep dependence upon God for every breath. I've gone through times of emotional weakness when I felt like I couldn't control my emotions or "snap out of it." So I cried to the Lord, and although my circumstances didn't change, my soul began to stabilize. I experienced "the carrying grace of God," and truly felt beneath me the everlasting arms.

It is in times of darkness that you learn something about "Him who is from the beginning."

Bible Examples

Many people in Bible times experienced dark seasons in God. These are but a few:

- Job. All his possessions and livelihood were taken from him in a single day, along with all his children. Then an awful disease attacked his entire body. The Book of Job chronicles his depression and bitterness of soul.
- Abraham. God promised Abraham a son, but not only was his wife, Sarah, barren, she was moving past her childbearing years. For twenty-five years Abraham and Sarah lived in the darkness of unfulfilled promises.
- Jacob. Jacob had the birthright and the blessing, but was consigned to fourteen years of servitude for his wives. After being double-crossed repeatedly, and being forced to sneak away secretly from his father-in-law, his darkness culminated in an all-night struggle with an angel.
- Joseph. Destined for great things, Joseph held onto a God-given dream. But he was sold unjustly into slavery, cut off from his family in a strange land, and after serving faithfully he was unjustly incarcerated in a dark, morbid Egyptian dungeon. Psalm 105:19 in speaking of this period in Joseph's life says, "The word of the Lord tested him."
- Moses. He had the calling, the gifting, the education, and the willingness to be God's man. But instead he ended up spending forty dark years — think of it, forty years — on the back side of the desert.
- Naomi. Her husband made her move to Moab during

a time of famine, and then while in Moab she buried her husband and her two sons. Naomi returned to Bethlehem in bitterness of soul and abject defeat.

- David. By the Spirit of God he killed the lion and the bear, and then killed the giant. He served Saul faithfully, and was even anointed by Samuel to be the next king of Israel. But rather than receiving the kingdom, he ended up running as a fugitive for his life from King Saul, living in caves and wilderness areas. Many of David's psalms express the passion of his soul during this dark period.

- Jesus. For thirty painful years, being full of godly insight and wisdom and revelation, He graciously kept silent. Then, when His time came, He was driven by the Spirit into the wilderness where He was tempted for forty dark days and nights.

Every one of these biblical characters were godly, holy, anointed people who were strong in faith, strong in the word, and strong in the Holy Spirit. But they all went through the valley of the shadow of death, experiencing seasons of darkness that broke, crushed, and squeezed their souls.

The Common Denominator

And there is one other element they all shared. There is this one common denominator in the outcome of their season of darkness: In each case, they entered into a new dimension of "spiritual fatherhood." Let me remind you of each circumstance:

- Job. After his trial, he became *father* again to seven sons and three daughters, he saw his children and grandchildren for four generations, and his influence in his generation was greatly multiplied.

- Abraham. After twenty-five years of holding to the promise of God, he finally became the *father* of Isaac.

- Jacob. He wrestled with God and prevailed — at which time he was renamed "Israel," the *father* of the twelve tribes.

- Joseph. After his slavery and imprisonment, he was promoted by God to a place of *fatherhood* over the entire Egyptian nation, as well as his father's family.
- Moses. After forty dark years in the desert, he was called of God to be a spiritual *father* to the entire Israelite nation.
- Naomi. After losing everything, Naomi became (through her daughter-in-law Ruth) the *mother* of one of the ancestors of Jesus Christ — Obed, grandfather of David.
- David. Although David probably felt ready years earlier, it was only after seven years of living as a fugitive from Saul that David was brought into the position of being the *father* (king) of the nation.
- Jesus. It was not until after His temptation that He was allowed to minister the *Father* heart of God to this planet.

Do you see it? Perhaps now you can better understand why many pastors, leaders, and churches in our nation have been going through seasons of inexplicable difficulty and crisis. God is preparing His Church for a new dimension of spiritual fatherhood.

What Now?

Well, what are we to do during this interim period? While we're waiting for a new dynamic of fatherhood to be manifest, how should we set our focus? The answer is in the title of this book: We are to abide in the presence of Jesus, giving ourselves to prayer, worship, praise, and intercession, setting our faces steadfastly to gaze upon His countenance until He comes to us. In short, remain in His face.

St. John of the Cross wrote about all this, describing it as "the dark night of the soul." He offered this counsel to those who find themselves in that place: "The way in which they are to conduct themselves in this night is not to devote themselves to reasoning and meditation, since this is not the time for it, but to allow the soul to remain in peace and quietness, although it may seem clear to them that they are doing nothing, and are wasting their time, and although it may appear to them that it is because of their weakness that they have no desire to think of anything. The truth is that they will be doing quite sufficient if they have patience and persevere in prayer without making any effort."

The Product: Spiritual Children

Finally, let me remind you of the product of spiritual fatherhood — spiritual children. God is preparing us for parenthood simply because He is preparing an unparalleled harvest.

Reinhardt Bonnke has said that the gospel is like an explosive, and intercession is the detonator. Preaching without intercession is like an explosive without a detonator, and intercession without an evangelistic thrust is like sparks with no dynamite. God is preparing a people of His presence who will be ready to accept the responsibilities of parenthood when God's Spirit ignites the harvest.

Maybe you, like me, feel a lot like Jacob right now. I'm wrestling with God, and darkness is all around. I don't understand God's purposes, or where things are going from here. But I've decided that I'm going to wrestle with God until dawn breaks. "I'm not letting go, God, until You bless me."

Order Form

Books by Bob Sorge

	Qty.	Price	Total
BOOKS:			
MINUTE MEDITATIONS	_____	$12.00	_____
OPENED FROM THE INSIDE: Taking the Stronghold of Zion	_____	$11.00	_____
IT'S NOT BUSINESS, IT'S PERSONAL	_____	$10.00	_____
POWER OF THE BLOOD: Approaching God with Confidence	_____	$13.00	_____
UNRELENTING PRAYER	_____	$13.00	_____
ENVY: THE ENEMY WITHIN	_____	$12.00	_____
LOYALTY: The Reach of the Noble Heart	_____	$14.00	_____
FOLLOWING THE RIVER: A Vision for Corporate Worship	_____	$10.00	_____
SECRETS OF THE SECRET PLACE	_____	$15.00	_____
Secrets Of The Secret Place COMPANION Study Gude	_____	$11.00	_____
Secrets Of The Secret Place LEADERS MANUAL	_____	$ 5.00	_____
GLORY: When Heaven Invades Earth	_____	$10.00	_____
PAIN, PERPLEXITY & PROMOTION	_____	$14.00	_____
THE FIRE OF GOD'S LOVE	_____	$13.00	_____
THE FIRE OF DELAYED ANSWERS	_____	$14.00	_____
IN HIS FACE: A Prophetic Call to Renewed Focus	_____	$13.00	_____
EXPLORING WORSHIP: A Practical Guide to Praise and Worship	_____	$16.00	_____
Exploring Worship WORKBOOK & DISCUSSION GUIDE	_____	$ 5.00	_____
DEALING WITH THE REJECTION AND PRAISE OF MAN	_____	$10.00	_____

SPECIAL PACKET
Buy one each of all Bob's books, and save 30%.
Call or visit our website for a current price.

Subtotal _____

Shipping, Add 10% (Minimum of $4.00) _____

Missouri Residents Add 7.725% Sales Tax _____

Total Enclosed (Domestic Orders Only/U.S. Funds) _____

Send payment with order to: Oasis House
P.O. Box 522
Grandview, MO 64030

Name _____

Address: Street _____

City _____ State_____Zip _____

For quantity discounts and MasterCard/VISA or international orders, call
816-767-8880 or order on our fully secure website: *www.oasishouse.com*.
See our site for free sermon downloads.